To my good friend
and mentor David,

Let's never stop
doing "good work"...
and let's do it
better!

Sam

What some people are saying about *Good Work Done Better*

"I met Sam Watts several years ago when, as Mayor, I proposed a high-priority plan to end homelessness in our city. The great Maya Angelou once said that "people will forget what you said and people will forget what you did, but people will never forget how you made them feel." I truly believe that Sam has a great impact on people because of his values, his altruism and his humanity. He leaves no one indifferent. When a person decides to give back to the community by placing their experience and talents at the service of the less fortunate it is commendable. Sam has taken a further step by encouraging us to change the way we think about the community-based non-profit sector. He also offers a breath of fresh air and new ideas for those who work in the sector and are seeking better outcomes and lasting solutions. *Good Work Done Better* is a must read."

—The Honourable Denis Coderre, Mayor of Montreal from 2013-2017. Denis served from 1997 to 2013 as the Member of Parliament for the riding of Bourassa in the Canadian House of Commons and held a number of different ministerial portfolios in the governments of Jean Chrétien and Paul Martin.

"I can vouch for the principles, orientations, and pointers contained in this book. They have been applied in my own organization for the past decade and I can confirm they work. They move the yardsticks. They make us stronger. They challenge, enlighten, and engage. Community organizations have an obligation and an accountability to those we serve and to those who choose to support us whether they are donors, foundations, or public institutions. Take Sam's book and run with it! You won't be sorry."

—Matthew Pearce, President and CEO, Old Brewery Mission. A recognized leader in the Montreal community, Matthew has been the CEO of OBM for more than twelve years and has also served on a variety of boards in the non-profit sector.

"Community-based non-profit organizations operate on a daily basis in our society, grappling with difficult social problems and trying to serve vulnerable people in our midst. As a rule, they rarely find the time to step back and reflect on their mission and their outcomes. Sam Watts believes this must change, and in this insightful book proposes many avenues to improve how CBNPs operate. He calls for an end to "patch work" charitable efforts, and calls for a much stronger emphasis on research and outcomes if we are going to achieve lasting change. This book should be read by all who work and volunteer in these organizations and those people interested in finding solutions to the social issues we face."

> —Geoff Kelley, former Minister for Aboriginal Affairs (2005-2007, 2011-12, and 2014-2018). Geoff was elected to seven consecutive mandates as a Member of the Quebec National Assembly for the riding of Jacques-Cartier from 1994-2018.

"As the leader of a community organization, my experience is that putting the principles in place that Sam Watts has outlined in **Good Work Done Better** *guarantees significant, positive and measureable impacts and outcomes. We need to be bold and Sam puts forward bold solutions for us to embrace. Community Based Non-Profits are quick to address societal gaps, but slow to change many of their own practices, even though a change of practices would more effectively impact client outcomes. We have traditionally been rooted in volunteerism, but we operate in continually changing and evolving environments and need to be nimble in order to adapt. CBNPs are regularly publicly criticized if they are not perceived to be doing more with less. In no other sector are organizations expected to operate in starvation cycles, and, in fact, are rewarded for doing so. This has had an enormous impact on how we are perceived by the public, media, donors, influencers and decision makers. It negatively affects our ability to achieve meaningful and lasting results for those we assist. Our traditional reliance on government funding, with philanthropic help to fully address the needs of our client bases, often puts us in a "master-servant" relationship that is detrimental to achieving outcomes needed to do the right thing – which in some cases means putting ourselves out of business because we've solved the issue. We need to be unapologetic about resourcing our sector properly and putting people in positions with the appropriate skills and abilities to solve these issues, as opposed to being satisfied with band aid solutions. It's the only way that we that will improve the lives of those we assist; those who need us the most."*

> —Deirdre Freiheit, President & CEO Shepherds of Good Hope and Shepherds of Good Hope Foundation, a well-respected community-based non-profit serving the city of Ottawa

"Good Work Done Better is required reading for any member of the media who wants to have a better understanding of how community-based non-profit organizations operate as well as to better understand the challenges these organizations face. Sam Watts presents solutions to long-standing problems that are well reasoned, well argued, and make sense. I hope that people read this book and see that change for the better is possible."

—Dave Kaufman, radio host, CJAD 800 and creator of the Kaufman podcasts

"Good Work Done Better respectfully challenges many of our preconceived ideas and invites us to examine a fresh approach – one that will help us address the complex social problems of the 21st century. Sam Watts invites us to reconsider a variety of assumptions about the way the community-based non-profit sector should operate. He also provides some interesting, actionable ideas. These ideas will help everyone who cares about the vulnerable and disenfranchised to move away from a purely charitable approach and move towards a problem-solving approach. My personal favourite was the key takeaway from the "Good Samaritan" story. Addressing a crisis isn't enough! To be truly helpful we must accompany those in need to a safer place and provide for a continuum of care"

—Sybil Dahan, President, Altius Healthcare. Chair of the Board of ANEB, a community-based non-profit organization that provides support for people who struggle with eating disorders

"I routinely get to observe hundreds of community-based non-profit leaders doing faith-focused work in the social justice sector. Sam Watts is one of them—but he is in a special class. Sam "gets it" on a completely different level. He understands that life transformation efforts must supersede disaster-relief work. He grasps the importance of collaboration without compromise in community initiatives. I have observed first-hand what's happening at Welcome Hall Mission. It's quite amazing. Sam pulls in the interest of politicians and patrons and people from every walk who want to help because he pushes the envelope with his honest assessments and creative solutions. And now, **Good Work Done Better** *puts it all out there for others who want to follow a similar path to serving the poor and powerless."*

—John Ashmen, President and CEO of Citygate Network. Founded in 1913, headquartered in Colorado, it has 300 member organizations across North America. Annually, its members serve approximately 66 million meals, provide more than 20 million nights of shelter and housing, and assist some 45,000 people in finding employment.

GOOD WORK DONE BETTER

Improving the Impact of
Community-Based Non-Profits

Sam Watts

 FriesenPress

Suite 300 - 990 Fort St
Victoria, BC, V8V 3K2
Canada

www.friesenpress.com

Copyright © 2020 by Sam Watts
First Edition — 2020

All rights reserved.

No part of this publication may be reproduced in any form, or by any means, electronic or mechanical, including photocopying, recording, or any information browsing, storage, or retrieval system, without permission in writing from FriesenPress.

ISBN
978-1-5255-6535-9 (Hardcover)
978-1-5255-6536-6 (Paperback)
978-1-5255-6537-3 (eBook)

1. *Social Science, Philanthropy & Charity*

Distributed to the trade by The Ingram Book Company

TABLE OF CONTENTS

xi	**Foreword**
1	**Introduction**
7	**Chapter 1** We do really, really good work—why change?
27	**Chapter 2** Can an "ah-ha moment" change your life?
39	**Chapter 3** Who is my neighbour?
53	**Chapter 4** What myths need to be exposed?
71	**Chapter 5** Are there some prevailing misunderstandings about community-based non-profit organizations?
89	**Chapter 6** Why does leadership matter?
101	**Chapter 7** Why do many boards of community-based non-profits miss the mark?
127	**Chapter 8** Can community organizations become the disruptors rather than the disrupted?
143	**Chapter 9** Where are the opportunities?
159	**Afterword**
161	**Appendix 1**
163	**Appendix 2** What can governments do? Three possible policy initiatives
167	**Appendix 3** Developing an actionable checklist
171	**Appendix 4** Is a Pandemic a Potential Disruptor?
175	**Acknowledgements**
177	**About the Author**

This book is dedicated to the courageous people who struggle with the realities of discrimination, violence, isolation, and poverty, and to the caring people who steadfastly meet them where they are and shine a helpful light on the pathway ahead.

FOREWORD

Dr. Karl Moore, Associate Professor, Desautels Faculty of Management, McGill University, Associate, Green Templeton College, Oxford University

The world is facing huge problems, like climate change, rising inequity, and poverty. These problems cannot be solved by one part of society working alone. Business, governments, and civil society must work together if the world is going to address these complex issues. My McGill University colleague and leading management thinker Henry Mintzberg argues that business is very effective at what it does, but it focuses on providing profits for its owners as its central goal, even in a world of increasing attention to corporate social responsibility. Government can be effective in addressing some things, however politics and getting re-elected is a key driver in most democracies. In many parts of the world, we are seeing "populists" and "strong men" hold onto power. To provide a needed balance, the third sector, or what Henry calls the "plural sector", must increasingly take its place alongside the private and public sector as the world seeks to respond to what seems to be almost intractable problems.

The world needs civil society even more than in the past, so the timing of this book is impeccable. In business, we have seen most industries and corporations facing business model disruption as new competitors enter industries and reinvent them. This "Uberization" of the world has made business today, for most firms and most industries, quite different than even a short decade ago. Government has also had to change how it goes about its work, though to a lesser degree. Civil society has changed the least in the last decade or two. This book does an important service by focusing on a central actor in civil society, community-based non-profit organizations (CBNPs), and how they could be reinvented to better serve.

Without a doubt, these organizations have done great work for many years, for many decades, serving the disadvantaged in our society; people who remain underserved and misunderstood by our societies. The people in these community-based non-profits have worked long, underpaid, if paid at all, hard hours. We must applaud them—they deserve our unreserved praise.

However, what Sam Watts cogently argues in this book is that the sector needs to change to realign itself towards solutions rather than mere "patches". In the last couple of decades, particularly the last decade, so much has changed in North American society. Technology has brought phones and many of us are glued to them for hours a day. We have the ability to summon a ride-sharing service, order a meal, and talk for free to friends halfway around the world. Most of us watch Netflix rather than old-fashioned television, we travel the world in a way that our parents never dreamed of, and we shop online rather than going to the mall. In a world characterized by the speed of change, Sam argues that community-based non-profit organizations need to change in order to serve their clients and communities. This is not just a theoretical argument based on what should be, it is based on Sam's rolling up his sleeves the last three years as the CEO of a critical CBNP, Welcome Hall Mission in Montreal, and working closely with other CBNPs to rethink their services. He concludes that most organizations on the front lines must make important shifts in order to continue their valuable and very important work.

CBNPs seldom work in isolation but often are funded by government. Sam argues for better alignment of government policy and programs that provide public funds to social efforts. Additionally, *Good Work Done Better* asks the general public, a key financial partner of many social causes, to reconsider the way they think and act.

At the core of this book is Sam's observation that he has observed an inadequate response to the voices of the vulnerable from the dedicated people who are trying to help them. He points out that this inadequacy is not due to an absence of compassion. It is due to a deficient model of service that isn't designed to resolve the evolving social challenges of the 21st century. In business and government we have seen disruption occurring; this book suggests that disruption is inevitable in the CBNP space. Sam draws on his twenty-five years of experience in the business world and argues that CBNPs can (and must) rethink their "business" models. He concludes that all of us—everyone who takes an interest in resolving the challenges of the vulnerable in society—can do considerably better. This is good news indeed.

Of course, one size does not fit all community-based non-profits, as Sam readily acknowledges, but I believe there are quite substantive questions that Sam raises based on real-work experience that are very helpful ones for leaders and boards of CBNPs to consider.

This is an important book not only for the NGO sector, but also for our societies. In a world characterized by inequality, discrimination, and racism, there are considerable parts of our societies that need help. Sam Watts convincingly argues that a central part of the NGO sector, community-based non-profit organizations, can up their game and contribute even more than in the past: Great people doing great things that can do even greater things. Read this book if you are one of the millions of people who work or volunteer in the sector or if you are someone who believes that the major social challenges of our time can be solved.

INTRODUCTION

Either write something worth reading or do something worth writing.
—Benjamin Franklin

The dominant voices in our world are the voices of the privileged. The disenfranchised do not control the public discourse. We have learned to expect that those on the margins will be ignored. However, for the past few years, I have had the awesome privilege of working closely with an incredible team of people who serve those who are living precariously. As a result, I am learning to listen to an alternative narrative. I have heard voices that speak from a place of disconnectedness and pain. At the same time, I have observed an inadequate response to those voices from the dedicated people who are trying to help them. This inadequacy is not due to an absence of compassion. It is due to deficiencies in the model of service. It is a model that emerged in the late 19th century but is not designed to resolve the evolving social challenges of the 21st century.

The aim of this book is to ask questions, raise issues, and propose fresh ways to think about how we should all respond to vulnerable people in our communities. Most human beings want to respond in a caring way, but for far too long "charitable" actions have been guided by beliefs that are not anchored in a robust understanding of the realities of the people who need help. Acting with charitable intentions is often more about the donor's feelings than it is about the true needs of the people who the donor aims to assist. This book will touch on some explanations for these incomplete understandings. One of the persistent reasons is that most of those who want to help the disadvantaged and the vulnerable are not well enough informed about the challenges. Another reason is that there is a fair amount of media glorification of a phenomenon that is best defined as a "random act of charity"—these efforts are sometimes individually commendable and, other times, badly misguided. The common denominator is that they do not fundamentally address the essence of the issue in question.

As we completed the final editing of this book we were living in the beginning stages of the challenges of COVID-19 in North America. The book is not intended to conduct an analysis of the response to this pandemic. It is far too early for that and undoubtedly thousands of scholarly articles and books will be written on the topic. Still, the point that Dr. Karl Moore emphasizes in his foreword may be worth noting. Specifically, that disruption in the "charitable" sector is inevitable. Will this pandemic be the disruptive catalyst for a sector that is operating in a less than optimal manner in its present form? That isn't clear yet, however, we have added a short appendix to this book to highlight several key points that merit consideration.

The primary focus of this book is local and regional organizations that directly provide hands-on help and care to vulnerable people groups. For the purposes of this book, these are called "**community-based non-profits**" or **CBNPs**. CBNPs are active at a grass-roots level in the community and are typically local in their scope. They may receive some government funding, but they are typically fuelled by donations and depend heavily on volunteer labour or underpaid employees. While these community-based non-profit organizations are ubiquitous, they do not receive the majority of tax-deductible donations within the overall non-profit sector. In Canada, they represent less than 20% of all donations, according to data compiled in 2010.[1]

In the broadest possible context, charities include a wide range of organizations, most of which are not the focus of this book. Generally speaking, if an organization can issue tax receipts in exchange for a donation, it is considered a charity. Therefore, charities include fundraising consolidators or charitable organizations that exist uniquely to collect funds and distribute them to other charities (like the United Way, for example). There are also thousands of private foundations, university and hospital foundations, religious orders or institutions, international aid organizations, human rights advocates, animal welfare, and hundreds of medically oriented charities that raise funds to conduct research into diseases, syndromes, or conditions. Charitable giving, overall, totalled more than 410 billion dollars in the USA in 2017, representing 2.1% of GDP,[2] with the overwhelming majority of all donations going to religious institutions, healthcare-related charities, and education. While this book challenges some preconceived notions that exist relating to philanthropy in general, its scope does **not** include the vast majority of these charitable organizations.

The observations and comments in this book take aim at the local non-profit efforts that directly address complex social conditions like poverty, hunger, homelessness, violence, or discrimination. These organizations usually serve a narrowly defined clientele within a specific city or region. The common denominator is that they advocate for, run, or oversee programs on the ground in a community or series of communities in an effort to address a particular problem or a variety of interrelated social conditions. Over the course of the 20th century, some North American community organizations that began rather modestly have grown to become sizeable entities. Some have adopted internal management structures that are similar to those found in major corporations.

The book will call into question many of the practices of a variety of "charitable organizations," as well as the donors and stakeholders that support them. Some CBNPs are tiny, with virtually no significant budgets, while others raise tens of millions of dollars to fund their activities. Very few of them find their way onto a list of well-recognized charities. Most are only known inside the circle of people they serve, within the region where they operate. The hardworking people who serve in these organizations are usually fiercely devoted to the admirable causes they seek to address, and they are paid far less than what they ought to be paid. The bulk of the work in many community-based non-profits is accomplished by armies of dedicated volunteers who devote thousands of hours annually to their causes. These organizations are, in turn, usually overseen by a volunteer board of directors.

The looming threat that these organizations must address is that they are clinging to strategies and models of service that are anchored in the past. If they do not change, they risk being disrupted by changes outside their control. The world has evolved, and these organizations that are seeking to address pressing social concerns of the 21st century are stuck in a bygone era, doing what they have always done, and oblivious to a variety of opportunities for improvement. They may be passionate about helping disadvantaged people improve, but many have not done enough to initiate systemic and organizational improvement of their own. How will people in need be served effectively if those who seek to serve them are resistant to improvement?

> How will people in need be served effectively if those who seek to serve them are resistant to improvement?

How can a historical attachment to a "handout approach" change to a data-driven, problem-solving approach anchored in best practices and innovation?

The chapters that follow will highlight myths and misconceptions that exist in the public domain. Given that the public-at-large is not exposed on a day-to-day basis to the challenges of the disadvantaged, how can they be expected to change their perspective and their responses when the community-based non-profit organizations themselves are trapped in incorrect assumptions? It would be like asking someone who is not a firefighter to be fully conversant in modern tactics for fire suppression, while the local fire department acts as if a good old bucket brigade is the most advanced technology in firefighting.

All is not as it should be in the world of community-based non-profits. There is something dreadfully wrong when community service organizations are more accountable to their donors than they are to those who require their services. We should be concerned that many of the worthy organizations that compete to attract our attention are making very little measurable progress. Success for a non-profit organization should mean that its existence eventually becomes unnecessary. There is something disquieting when the social pages of the newspaper feature beautiful people posing in black dresses or tuxedos at a glittering charity event. Parties are not wrong, nor is fundraising. Dinners, golf tournaments and casino nights are ubiquitous in charitable circles. However, we should be concerned if such events are more beneficial to the attendees than they are to the people that a front-line community organization seeks to serve. Do lavish events attract attention to a worthy cause or are they inefficient fundraising exercises—and possibly a bit self-indulgent? Are North American tax laws constructed appropriately? For example, is it acceptable that a $1000 donation to an exclusive private school's foundation produces the same net effect on a donor's taxes as a $1000 donation given to a shelter that exists to help women escape violence or sex trafficking? These are just a few of hundreds of questions that we need to ask.

The CBNPs that are the focus of this book seek to address a variety of societal tragedies and unacceptable realities. Poverty, discrimination, disenfranchisement, disconnection and addiction are like thieves. They leave a trail of victims and create collateral damage. They handicap individuals and limit their ability to achieve their full potential. They often sideline a percentage of our population, limiting their contribution to society. They also affect future generations because children who grow up experiencing poverty or trauma are less likely to succeed. Those who enjoy lives of relative privilege ought to respond with horror at individual instances of egregious social calamity. Often, we merely shake our head and feel frustrated, or we try to do something that we think is helpful. In fairness, we often do not know how to help even when we feel like we ought to help. At the same time, a comprehensive solution-oriented approach eludes us.

> Poverty, discrimination, disenfranchisement, disconnection, and addiction are like thieves. They leave a trail of victims and create collateral damage.

The basic service model that is being deployed by community-based non-profit organizations to address complex social conditions has not changed for 50 years, yet the nature of the social conditions and the construct of society has changed dramatically in that time. There have been enormous societal changes in the late 20th and early 21st centuries. The way that everyone lives, works, and interacts has changed enormously since the beginning of the 1960's, and there have been even more ground-breaking changes in technology since the turn of the century. Yet many parts of the community-based non-profit sector continue to function with a mindset that is firmly anchored in a bygone era. In some cases, 19th century solutions are being cheerfully offered to respond to 21st century needs.

Community-based non-profit organizations have a history of leading the charge against injustice. They have challenged a culture that allowed, even encouraged, behaviours that most people find reprehensible in the 21st century. These groups have been tireless in caring for the downtrodden, advocating for those with no voice, and providing hope to those who had lost it.

I love and deeply value the energy and passion of the CBNP sector. I am an unrepentant believer in the essential role that these thousands of organizations play in addressing the social challenges and the historical inequalities of the disadvantaged, the abused, and the disconnected within North American society.

> Nineteenth-century solutions are being cheerfully offered to respond to 21st century needs.

Is the working model of CBNPs broken? Perhaps, but that does not mean that the work being done is of no value. Can this sector reform itself? Yes, it can. Many organizations in this sector have taken major steps towards reform. Is there a way to ensure that organizations that aim to serve the most vulnerable and disadvantaged are appropriately led, governed, and resourced? Of course there is. However, the process of reform is never easy. Disruption may or may not precede reform. Disruption could take the form of a radical shift in government policy. For example, should the federal government introduce a game-changing policy like a guaranteed minimum income, such an initiative might make some CBNPs unnecessary. Disruption can also occur due to structural or funding shifts in the sector or if some existing organizations in the sector radically alter the playing field.

Some may ask: Why not write a book about the ineffectiveness or inadequacies of government-led efforts or the reality that most policy-driven efforts in North America have been either unfocused or grossly underfunded? The answer is twofold. First, governments are easy targets. There is little disagreement that, in many jurisdictions, there has been a lack of coordination between various levels of government and that their social policies and funding priorities have been, for the most part, incoherent. One of the problems is that elections are not won or lost based on having a robust set of policy ideas that are designed to combat discrimination, kids who go to school hungry, or housing for those experiencing homelessness. More importantly, the social and societal challenges we face in the 21st century cannot be remedied by government action alone. Policy makers have a critically important role to play, but the complexities of implementation are challenging if there is a lack of alignment due to turf wars and bureaucratic processes. The consequence has been that policy makers have become addicted to funding quick and easy patches that obscure issues without resolving the core challenges. In other words, money is typically being invested to obscure the evidence of the problem but very little investment is allocated to the longer term work of addressing the root of major social challenges.

There are also obstacles within the network of community-based non-profit organizations that need to be removed so that those in need can be served with dignity and efficiency. New government programs or resources will produce little meaningful impact if the funds are spread out across thousands of well-meaning organizations to maintain "great programs" with noble ambitions, especially those that are not linked to measurable outcomes. Another hard truth is that making more money available for CBNPs will not solve any problems if the CBNPs are not managing their existing resources effectively.

The good news is that change is coming. The bad news is that the challenges associated with the coming changes are not going to be easy to digest. The CBNPs that deliver services on the front lines will have to change how they respond. Governments, the public, funders, the media will all need to re-think many beliefs and assumptions. When that happens, it will become possible to help donors, supporters, and stakeholders understand that good work on its own is never good enough. Good work can be done better.

1. https://www150.statcan.gc.ca/n1/pub/11-008-x/2012001/t/11637/tbl05-eng.htm

2. https://www.charitynavigator.org/index.cfm?bay=content.view&cpid=42

CHAPTER 1
We do really, really good work—why change?

Confidence is the prize given to the mediocre.
—Robert Hughes

When an organization is doing good work, why not leave it alone? What kind of daft, insensitive individual would dare to question good work? With all that is wrong in the world, why would someone who serves in the non-profit sector write about the opportunities for improvement in the fine community-based organizations that are devoted to serving people in need? These questions deserve an answer before we continue.

I have the incredible privilege of serving in a community-based non-profit organization (CBNP). People frequently tell our team members that they are kind and generous. A frequently repeated phrase is, "You do good work." There are times when random people stop me on the street to compliment me personally on the work our organization is doing. While this is nice feedback, it tends to make people like me believe that our organization must be doing work that is utterly beyond reproach. It can become a prevailing narrative; one that provides a heightened degree of confidence—even if you really are somewhat mediocre. When everybody tells you that you are wonderful, you tend to believe it, and it becomes an important component of organizational validation.

When we keep hearing, "You do good work," a better response might be to pause and wonder if the good work we are doing is the very best work that can be done. Are we as good as we think we are, or is there significant room for improvement in our structures, leadership, programs, and processes? Are we merely putting gravel in the recurring potholes on a road that was improperly constructed and should be completely rebuilt? Is the work we are doing serving our clients, or are we merely giving our volunteers a feeling of satisfaction? Are we caught in a routine where we are systematically doing things that have outlived their usefulness? Have we properly framed the issues that we seek to address? Are we able to measure the outcomes that we say we are seeking to achieve, or are we merely responding to urgencies? Are we truly making a difference and helping people change their trajectories? We may THINK we are doing good work, but what if we aren't?

One reality of front-line work with disadvantaged and disconnected people is that outreach-oriented organizations can become so absorbed by the day-to-day problems that confront them that they lack the time and perspective to truly assess their effectiveness. CBNPs tend to work in the middle of the problem, rather than on the problem. When most of the people in the organization are dealing with the crisis directly in front of them, it is relatively easy for the organization itself to become part of the problem while being utterly convinced that everyone in the organization is doing essential work and that the world would collapse if the services of the organization ceased to exist. In psychology, this is sometimes called cognitive blindness—a phenomenon that occurs when someone is intensely focused on one set of circumstances and completely misses seeing some other obvious element.

> Community-based non-profit organizations tend to work in the middle of the problem, rather than on the problem.

Every community service organization tends to believe two things: One, that the organization has a reasonably thorough understanding of the problem it is trying to address, and, two, that their clients would be in a far worse position if it ceased to exist. Many services are badly needed, but no organization is indispensable. Most community organizations are trying to resolve problems that desperately cry out to be resolved. The question is: Do their strategies and activities produce outcomes that measurably change the scope of the problem? Are the tactics actually altering the social landscape of the city or the region?

We may all agree that the motives of CBNPs are fundamentally pure. Most are trying their level best to solve pervasive social challenges. Very few organizations that serve the vulnerable do so with an eye to personal gain. Almost none have any evil intentions. The problem is that good intentions do not always translate into appropriate actions, and noble efforts do not necessarily result in the improvements or produce the changes that everyone claims to be pursuing.

> Good intentions do not always translate into appropriate actions. Noble efforts do not necessarily result in improvements.

It might seem unkind to scrutinize a sector where so many selfless people sacrifice time and money to care for the least fortunate, the excluded, and the disenfranchised. However, the sector itself is far too large to ignore. The non-profit sector is, if consolidated, one of the larger economic sub-sectors in North America. In the USA, the entire non-profit sector accounts for approximately 12.3 million jobs representing 10.2% of private sector employment.[1] Non-profit organizations also attract highly engaged volunteers. A large percentage of people living in North America claim that they put in regular volunteer time with a non-profit effort in their community. According to the National Center for Charitable Statistics, there are well in excess of one and a half million registered non-profit organizations in the United States of America.[2]

Interestingly, those who have studied non-profits agree that the sector is also one of the least understood. Additionally, the sub-sector that is the focus of this book, community-based non-profit organizations (CBNPs), might be one of the least examined sectors. This is largely due to the high level of sensitivity associated with saying anything critical-sounding about any group trying to help the disadvantaged or vulnerable. Most people assume that the reflex of helping is a virtuous reflex. Almost everybody is quite happy that some group has stepped forward and is reaching out to respond to those who are marginalized or forgotten.

So if wonderful organizations are willing to try to provide the best help that they are able to provide, should we give these good-hearted organizations a free pass? If members of the public constantly congratulate the wonderful people who do such outstanding work in the community, but never scrutinize them, does it help alleviate the plight of vulnerable people who need help? Is everything that looks good, the right thing to do? Instead, is it more helpful to suggest that community-based non-profit organizations make critical changes in their governance, leadership, and operating models in order to achieve breakthroughs in responding to the challenges that are facing society?

In case there is any reason for doubt, this book intends to validate the need for community-based non-profits. They matter. They are essential to our communities. At the same time, anyone who truly cares about meeting the needs of the disadvantaged should be asking CBNPs to break away from their traditional ways of thinking.

> Is everything that looks good, the right thing to do?

This book proposes that seeking to address or resolve an injustice requires much more than nice people who will act with the very best of intentions. The trap of good intentions is that it can lead to gigantic blind spots. A CBNP can easily fall into practices that inadvertently undermine their stated objectives. Organizations that seek to correct injustices always firmly believe they are doing the right things. Their donors and stakeholders typically applaud them. Complimentary articles are written about them, highlighting their importance in the community. Client successes get attention and become legendary. Their Executive Directors are showered with awards for commitment and devotion to community work. Everyone loudly sings their praises. But what if nothing changes? What if the evidence shows that, in most cases, the Herculean efforts are not producing verifiable, tangible outcomes? What if the problems the organization is trying to address continue to grow? What should be done?

Full disclosure

I currently serve as CEO/Executive Director in a Montreal-based non-profit organization called Welcome Hall Mission, or Mission Bon Accueil in French. It is an enormous privilege to serve alongside an incredible group of passionate team members. It is a role that provides interesting insights into how the community-based non-profit sector works, or sometimes, does not work nearly as well as it ought to. I came to the non-profit world out of the private sector. My career included sales roles, marketing positions, and eventually management in organizations where the goal was to produce a return on investment for their shareholders. When I decided to leave the corporate world to start a consulting practice, it was with the aim of helping companies improve.

Consulting was so enjoyable that I was sure I'd found my calling. It was a great learning experience to spend fourteen years working with a wide variety of business organizations. My principal role in most assignments was to guide individual teams within an organization to align their efforts with each other so that they could produce better results and achieve improved financial outcomes. I look back on this work with tremendous satisfaction. The successes of ethically run enterprises that improve our lives with technological advances are at the heart of how progress occurs in our world. A well-run business can produce a return on investment for its shareholders and also be a catalyst for social progress.

With a few minor exceptions, my clients were businesses that were innovative and forward thinking. They were also organizations that paid their people well, and many were involved in charitable endeavours in their communities. I loved the work that I was doing and never contemplated working in the non-profit sector. It was not on my radar.

Then, one day, completely unexpectedly, a recruitment professional called to gauge my interest in leading one of our city's iconic non-profit organizations. I was surprised and a little less than enthusiastic at the onset. It is a lot of fun to work with diverse organizations and on a number of projects simultaneously. I had always maintained that I would never leave my consulting practice to take on any "real job" unless someone offered me an opportunity to change the world. I was quite certain that such an offer was not forthcoming.

This, it turns out, was a miscalculation on my part. In my mind, the opportunity to change the world might have included an offer from some revolutionary business start-up to lead a team that would disrupt the status quo. In mid-2016, the board of Welcome Hall Mission/Mission Bon Accueil asked me to lead that organization. It was, and is, an opportunity to change the world—or at least a small part of the world.

Welcome Hall Mission, founded in 1892, initially functioned as a downtown soup kitchen and para-church outreach, in response to growing social challenges in the city of Montreal. Interestingly, one of its first mission statements included the objective of "the prevention of cruelty to women and children." This statement stands as evidence of the radically progressive thinking that existed among the founders at a time when the primary emphasis in society revolved entirely around men.

Under the stewardship of my visionary predecessor, Cyril Morgan, the Mission grew from a small, one-dimensional entity into a well-respected powerhouse among community-based non-profits in our city. It expanded from having fewer than 35 staff team members to having over 140 full-time employees. Like many other similar organizations all over North America, it provides important services to people in need. These services include temporary shelter, permanent housing, meals, clothing, free dentistry, free grocery stores, and employment assistance. The organization serves men, women, youth, and families. The programs address gaps in the social safety net and meet needs that existing services within the medical network and the hospital system cannot provide efficiently to vulnerable groups in the population. The Mission enjoys considerable public and political support in the city of Montreal and is frequently invited to consult on matters of policy with various government ministries and government officials. Additionally, the people who work at the Mission are called upon by the media to comment on issues related to homelessness, housing, and food security. Still, everyone will freely admit that we do not have all the answers. Everyone is learning and evolving in their efforts to respond to the needs in the community. We routinely ask ourselves if we are doing the right things, and if we are doing them in the best possible way. A good example is the response to the issue of chronic homelessness.

The evolving reality of homelessness

Any community organization that operates an emergency shelter that serves people experiencing homelessness should be evaluating the extent to which they are part of the problem, or part of the solution. For the first hundred years or so of the existence of emergency shelters, a fundamental belief was that people who fell into homelessness were "poor lost souls" who needed to be rescued. The primary aim was to encourage these people to turn their lives around. The principal belief was that until a transient person changed their ways, it was unwise to help them regain housing. Labels such as incorrigibles, tramps, hobos, and misfits were hurled in their direction. They were often destined to wander from city to city and circulate in a network of emergency shelters or check in and out of various substandard rooming houses until they died.

The public generally held the view that these people were in this predicament because of a series of poor choices, and therefore, they had largely authored their own fate. In addition, they were misdiagnosed medically. Virtually nobody asked questions about issues arising from trauma, mental illness, and addiction. Sympathetic people pitied them, and more judgmental people dismissed their problems as a function of a prevailing human weakness. Those who struggled with addictions were treated like delinquents, sinners, and oddballs. My grandmother, a devoutly religious woman who grew up in the early part of the 20th century, referred to homeless men in casual conversation as "drifters," "drunks," "bums," and "ne'er-do-wells." She did not intend to insult anyone. She merely used language she had been taught, and she reflected a commonly held understanding of the era.

Rescue Missions, an early iteration of emergency shelters that served a number of urban centres in the early part of the 20th century, were a bit counter-cultural. They believed that people's lives could change. They also believed that the mechanics that led to a change involved a firm decision to pursue a rehabilitated lifestyle.

> Rescue Missions in the early part of the 20th century were counter-cultural. They believed that people's lives could change.

Depending on who was leading the effort, the definition of rehabilitation was somewhat fluid. The birth of organizations like Alcoholics Anonymous (AA) in the late 1930's introduced a different approach to the challenges of addiction. Despite this, and a mounting preponderance of research-based medical information, there are still North American emergency shelters that anchor their approach to rehabilitation on a mix of tough love and a defined spiritual change.

I firmly believe that a true change of heart coupled with the profound intention to change direction is a vital and powerful thing. I unapologetically subscribe to the unembellished Christian message of good news, hope, reconciliation, redemption, and liberty. In our North American context, many people who hit rock bottom will declare that their journey to wholeness and substantial life-change included a very emotional experience of personal conversion and spiritual change. Some say that it is the most transformative part of their personal journey. There is nothing quite as liberating as a deep and intensely personal redemptive experience. It can change a person who is filled with hate and self-loathing into a person who loves themselves and others. It can help set someone on a completely new course. However, any commitment to a new set of lifestyle choices has to include developing healthy connections in a family or a community. Additionally, the process of rehabilitation or life-change usually requires medical assistance or some counsel from an experienced and qualified professional social worker.

Recovery programs like AA include the acknowledgment of a higher power and the need for ongoing peer support because the founders of AA recognized that an addict needs a community. Anyone who has worked with the addicted or the abused recognizes that a return to physical and emotional health is usually a lengthy process, and a genuine religious conversion or other forms of personal renewal cannot be promoted as a magic cure. A change of heart does not erase medical conditions or remedy the deep psychological damage of the wounded. It does not instantly heal shattered relationships or eliminate the consequences of past actions.

Organizations that respond to people who are vulnerable or struggling with addictions, psychological wounds, or scars must ensure that the care is guided by well-trained people who have recognized professional credentials. Some organizations position themselves as responders to the disadvantaged, but they continue to employ unqualified or under-qualified people on the front lines. Well-meaning people who are under-equipped or unqualified can do a lot of damage while trying to help. Nobody would trust a dentist to design and build a bridge—or ask an engineer to perform a root canal. Yet, for many years, people who were not properly educated or trained often provided front-line care for the most disadvantaged people in our communities.

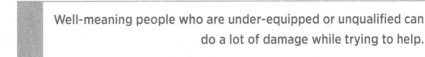

> Well-meaning people who are under-equipped or unqualified can do a lot of damage while trying to help.

People who have experienced trauma, rejection, and abuse do not respond well to an approach that undervalues the need for evidence-based medical therapy and appropriate psychological counselling.

Those who serve the vulnerable also have to be tuned in to the very real history of well-documented institutional excesses and unspeakable evils that have been perpetrated in the name of organized (or disorganized) religion. There are plenty of stories about abusive and unforgivable predatory behaviour of priests, ministers, and other authority figures. In some cases CBNPs had a practice of compelling the destitute to attend a religious service and profess allegiance to a particular belief in order to obtain a free meal or go to the front of the line. In other ways, many quasi-charitable organizations developed equally indefensible rules that treated those seeking service as if they were beggars. People who showed up for help were not always treated with the utmost care and dignity.

Designed for those in need?

Many CBNPs have allowed the adoption of practices that are more appealing to volunteers and donors than they are to the needs of the end-users. Those who give time to serve the disenfranchised (and those who are financial donors) can inadvertently become fixated on doing more of the same thing in the same way. Meanwhile, the people who receive the services may not be getting what they truly need. Still, the majority of clients will speak in favourable terms about the experience at a CBNP. Often, the clients or beneficiaries do not realize that they should expect something far better.

Every CBNP continues to be firmly convinced that they are doing exceptionally good work because the programs and facilities are always full and because, occasionally, an incredibly compelling and heart-warming story of miraculous life change happens. A courageous individual may emerge out of the cycle of poverty, abuse, or addiction and radically change within a short time period. These stories are not the norm; they are the exception. The norm is that the work of CBNPs is extremely difficult and there are many stories that are heartbreaking and mind-boggling. The process of change often takes years and includes steps forward, followed by multiple steps backward.

Many community organizations rely on good-hearted volunteers as the first line of care, and this has contributed to a culture that focuses on addressing immediate needs, rather than a strategy that aims to address the root of the problem. Why? Because donors and volunteers enjoy the experience of providing immediate assistance. It can be a bit of a rush and a feeling of real accomplishment when a volunteer serves a free meal, helps a child understand a math problem for the first time, or joins an intervention team that extracts a young woman from the control of a pimp and whisks her away to a safe location.

Events that address very visible problems or tragedies frequently generate dramatic stories and a groundswell of praise from supporters. They nourish the belief that any organization that feeds 15% more people or has 10% more visitors to its drop-in centre must be doing good work. However, are they addressing the real needs of the disadvantaged or merely responding with a temporary patch? By ensuring that the organization appeals to the emotional needs of volunteers and supporters are they failing to address the root of the challenge?

CBNPs carry on at length in their annual reports about how more resources are essential for them to continue to address emerging needs and fine-tune their financial appeals to donors in the hope that more money will be donated so that the efforts can continue. Unfortunately, a growing problem is not a reason to feel institutionally validated.

One changed life is a reason to celebrate. However, when the needs of the majority are not met, it is disingenuous to claim that the collective response to complex social challenges is adequate. Instead, the persistence of a problem ought to be a reason to ask some very pointed questions. Is it possible that some of the existing programs are enabling, perhaps even facilitating, the phenomenon that a specific CBNP seeks to eliminate? Is the "good work" that community groups are doing creating conditions that keep the challenge bubbling under the surface, but largely under control? Is the effort to "help" people resulting in a shallow definition of the word "help"? Is "help" more about the people who serve than it is about those who ought to be served?

Given these concerns, some CBNPs are taking a very hard look at what they are doing. Many are becoming more committed to providing better services. Most major North American CBNPs have hired professional, qualified staff and renovated their facilities. All of this is good. But the question remains: Was this real change, or were they just putting a coat of paint on an old, run-down building? Many organizations changed from an archaic "rules-based" approach in order to be more welcoming, and they started calling the people that they serve "clients" or "guests." However, the fundamentals of the model of service usually remain static.

> It is always hard to admit that we, the people doing the good work, are part of the problem.

Ultimately, progressive organizations (like the place where I serve) recognized that the historical approach was not fundamentally addressing the needs of the majority of the people who came to the door. Sure, everyone agreed that CBNPs were an essential service in the community. However, the help that was being offered was effectively putting a tiny bandage on a gigantic, festering wound. Ultimately, many CBNPs had to come to grips with the fact that realities had changed and the response, while always offered with generous intentions, was becoming less and less adequate. It is always hard to admit that we, the people doing the good work, are part of the problem. A CBNP that is not evolving will eventually discover that the problems it is trying to address will continue to grow. When the problems continue to grow, organizations that respond to the problem will be forced to expand their services, and unsatisfactory outcomes will continue to be the norm.

Wait! Didn't the organization where I serve obtain great results in the years between 1892 and 2000? Didn't our inner city Mission, and many others like us, help thousands of individuals towards legitimate life change over the years? Yes, there were quite a few success stories. Many of the success stories had a ripple effect; a phenomenon where one changed life altered the trajectory of hundreds of other lives. Many of these stories were dramatic and inspirational. It is important to acknowledge that many of our programs and services changed the course of events for many disadvantaged and disconnected people. Some former clients and beneficiaries can specifically point to a period of their life when they hit rock bottom, but thanks to the work of the dedicated staff or volunteers at a CBNP like ours, the trajectory of their life was altered.

> Every person is valuable, even if they have been robbed of their dignity or if they have made a series of suboptimal choices.

Every person is valuable, even if they have been robbed of their dignity or if they have made a series of suboptimal choices in life. Furthermore, none of us is immune from the potential to experience discrimination, violence, hunger, or poverty. It is clear that lives can change as a result of a singular act of kindness or intervention, no matter how misguided or under-informed that intervention may be. However, if a better response to complex social issues exists, does it make sense to carry on with practices that produce a number of limited positive outcomes but do not have any impact on the issues that are at the root of the problem?

How did change begin among organizations that respond to homelessness?

Curiously, the motivation to make radical changes in addressing the phenomenon of urban homelessness was not the result of external pressures. It did not come from governments, the medical community, the media, or donors. These stakeholders repeatedly told those who ran traditional emergency shelters what a great job they were doing. Surprisingly, the change was driven by the people working in traditional emergency shelters who were recognized as leaders in the field. It began with a commitment to gather real data, and then seek to understand it.

The data demonstrated that the majority of clients who find themselves experiencing homelessness simply require a little bit of short-term help, and that they are quite capable of re-orienting and redirecting themselves. A relatively small percentage of people who seek help at emergency shelters require access to important services in order to break habits, obtain medical treatment for mental illness, or address life-skills challenges that will allow them to emerge from a state of homelessness. This smaller percentage of clients face multi-dimensional challenges that cannot be resolved by quick, simple actions. The charitable, unconditional offer of a night of shelter was serving to prevent a person from being forced to sleep under an overpass, but a rules-based overnight shelter frequently did very little to help anyone avoid a lifestyle of isolation or chronic homelessness. More importantly, the longer someone circulated within a network of emergency shelters, cared for by concerned and well-meaning people, the more likely they were to develop an ongoing lifestyle of homelessness.

Collectively, society now understands a great deal more about mental illness, the struggles associated with addiction, and the psychological complexities of childhood or adolescent trauma or social exclusion. Still, the discovery that a major reason for the onset of addictive behaviour is related to pain or disconnection has still not met with broad acceptance, despite the publicity that surrounds the recent opioid crisis. This is partly because many of the treatment options for addiction are still centred on disciplines designed to produce lifestyle changes. Some approaches tend to overlook the fact that physical or psychological pain is an isolating phenomenon. The stories emerging from the current opioid crisis are a case in point. Significant numbers of reasonably well-adjusted people have spiralled out of control due to post-operative pain-reduction therapies that included the use of various opioids.

Some well-regarded researchers suggest that the opposite of addiction may not be sobriety. It is more likely "community" or a similar word. Canadian professor and psychologist Bruce K. Alexander has been instrumental in making a clear connection between compulsive addictive behaviour and disconnectedness. When asked about the realities of addiction in the 21st century in an article published in *The Sun* in March 2019, Dr. Alexander indicated that the research concludes that 75% of those who become addicted to a variety of substances can get over their addictions without much assistance. He also said:

> *Of the one-quarter who do not get over their addictions naturally, some die, and others stay in a cycle of recovery and relapse. This last group receives the most public attention. They fill self-help meeting rooms and treatment centres. A large percentage of this visible minority are resistant to treatment, which creates the illusion that addiction is an intractable, chronic disease. This supposed intractability is then used to explain the marginal success of treatment regimes. The field of addiction is stuck in endless debates about the merits of competing forms of treatment because it ignores the dilemmas human beings face in our fragmented world. Most alternative treatments also ignore this. For example, a number of*

nutrition experts claim that if we find the right supplements, we will no longer be troubled with addiction, depression, anxiety, and other ills. Likewise, there's the widespread promotion of mindfulness meditation, which says the fallible individual will be made stronger by esoteric practices. [3]

The study of neuroscience provides ample information that the reward circuitry in the brain of the addicted person makes environmental links. Dr. John Krystal, in a scientific study published in 2016, said: "The persistence and inflexibility of addiction-related associations are factors that trigger craving and relapse." Willpower on its own isn't an impediment to substance abuse. Relapses are exceedingly common. This is why people who struggle with addiction often ricochet from program to program in the hope of finding the elusive elixir that will propel them to recovery. In recent years, healthcare professionals have re-positioned drug and alcohol addiction as a health issue. Recently, prominent physicians, including Dr. Sandy Buchman, the President of the Canadian Medical Association, have called for the decriminalization of all drugs. He is not alone. A number of leaders in the medical community have concluded that addiction is more of a wellness issue than a criminal problem. An individual who is struggling with addictions and has experienced social exclusion will not "turn their life around" and achieve stability because they are put in prison. Drugs make their way into most jails and addictive behaviour is seldom changed by an extended stay in a correctional institution.

A bit of historical context

Anyone who has visited the extravagant mansions in Newport, Rhode Island will have witnessed some of the results of a period of unprecedented wealth generation in the United States. Writers have used unflattering terms like "robber baron capitalists" to describe the ruthlessness and acumen of entrepreneurs like the Vanderbilts, the Berwins, and their contemporaries to amass enormous amounts of money and power. Most newly wealthy capitalists built personal fortunes and felt compelled to develop a lifestyle that emulated many of the practices of European aristocracy. In his book, *The Theory of the Leisure Class*, sociologist and economist Thorstein Veblen called it "conspicuous consumption." Dr. Veblen suggested that it was not enough to have money and assets. He observed that the uber-wealthy of the era had to be seen to be relatively idle and actively spending in an ostentatiously wasteful manner in order to elevate their social status.

In the very same period, hundreds of non-profit organizations were founded all over North America. These social agencies emerged in the late 1800's through the early 1900's as a response to urgent needs linked to the squalid social conditions in rapidly growing cities. Many organizations enjoyed the financial backing of wealthy people. They addressed needs that were a persistent reality of that period. Some acted as advocates for social change, while others believed that their role was strictly to lessen the suffering of people who were considered "unfortunates." The leaders often possessed a unique combination of faith and social activism.

When a 21st-century mindset is superimposed, it is easy to be critical of the prevailing social perspectives of any bygone era. In order to be fair, it is important to understand that the public discourse around issues like poverty reduction or equality of opportunity was somewhat limited. Many wealthy people in the late 19th and early 20th centuries took little interest in those who were living on the margins and viewed them as little more than uneducated labourers who were not able to rise beyond their assigned station in the social order. In addition, governments did not have the revenue base to address social issues until well after the imposition of income taxes. The result was that most governments ignored many emerging social needs or considered them the domain of the church to resolve.

Consequently, hundreds of charitable services in North America came into being due to the advocacy of people who saw a problem that they felt they could not ignore. Many are still operating today. Some were affiliated, formally or informally, with Catholic or Protestant churches, and they drew volunteers, and a portion of their funding, from these institutions. Institutions led by people of faith and compassion were responsible for sensitizing society to the desperate situation of the underprivileged. Many of the leaders of this charitable movement were strong advocates of social change, and they lobbied governments for legislative changes. In time, some of these changes brought about improvements and altered the way social services were delivered by the middle part of the 20th century.

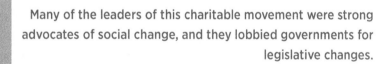

> Many of the leaders of this charitable movement were strong advocates of social change, and they lobbied governments for legislative changes.

The advent of the First World War, and the resulting political and social upheaval in the early part of the 20th century, contributed to a change in the collective consciousness in Europe and North America. The Great Depression of the 1930's exposed additional challenges. The rise of the labour movement resulted in a number of improvements for the working classes and eventually helped create a class of workers who were living above the poverty line. The Second World War and the post-war economic recovery provided additional fuel to an ongoing social evolution. Most liberal democratic states that emerged after the Second World War gradually assumed responsibility for many aspects of the social well-being of all citizens, and the modern "welfare state" came into being.

A welfare state may have emerged, but one of the more common social services that endured in most urban areas was an entity that became known as the local "Rescue Mission," mentioned earlier in this chapter. The major focus of these facilities was to provide homeless people with basic food and shelter. Additionally, the staff and volunteers provided some very basic counselling services that were designed to provide temporary guidance to those in need. A fair amount of effort centred on supplying a safe but temporary location for men who were considered "transient." They were encouraged to reform their bad habits, reconsider their personal responsibilities, and return to their families. Rescue Missions all over North America operated with a similar emphasis. Other social services that focused on the safety of women and children, provided care for those with special needs, or developed services tailored to the needs of communities of First Nations were founded in various cities but there was not a prevailing sense of urgency in the early part of the 20th century to address many of these specific concerns.

Several community organizations that began serving the public in an ad hoc manner have evolved to become professionally run service centres. Some continue to operate independently while others have created partnerships with government agencies. A few operate as extensions of specific church-related charitable efforts, while others are secular. Several have very narrow service offerings, while many others offer a multitude of community services. Transnational brands like the YMCA and the Salvation Army are examples of two legacy organizations that have evolved into large multiservice organizations.

One of the constant challenges is that organizations that aim to deliver front-line services to extremely vulnerable people usually struggle to obtain adequate funding to operate. A recent survey conducted by the Non-profit Finance Fund in the United States of America (there were over 5,000 respondents) found that 86% of non-profits believed that needs are rising, and 57% said that they did not have the capability or resources to meet these needs. The top challenge that they identified was a concern about their financial sustainability.[4] It is quite likely that their perceptions are correct. Those who serve the most vulnerable people in North America can quote statistics and studies that point to increased levels of poverty, lack of access to affordable housing, systemic discrimination, and a continuing cycle of violence directed at women. The need is growing and the available funding is not keeping pace. The United States of America continues to experience racial inequalities that produce collateral social problems, including the disproportionate number of African Americans who live in poverty or are incarcerated.

Canadians should not be too smug. One of the very worrying Canadian social issues is that the fastest growing sector of the population—those who identify among First Nations, Inuit, or Metis—are disproportionately the victims of violence, abuse, addiction, incarceration, and the experience of homelessness. Furthermore, the well-established philanthropic system in Canada is not easily accessible to (or understood by) indigenous communities. Even more worrying, according to the 2016 Census, indigenous children under the age of 14 make up 7.7% of the Canadian population, but 52.2% of children in foster care (aged 0-14) are indigenous. [5] This is scandalous and, if left unaddressed, has the potential to become a major social challenge in less than a generation. Action to respond to this emerging concern will be costly, but it will be exponentially costlier to do nothing about it.

When social challenges continue to persist, the community-based non-profit sector typically blames changing demographics, disruptions in family dynamics, or underlying local economic problems. A favourite reason, frequently cited, is insufficient government funding. Organizations delivering front-line social services will never say that they obtain enough government money to get the job done! Some groups are much more vocal than others in this regard, perhaps believing that the "squeaky wheel gets the grease." This tactic has sometimes been successful. Community organizations that are very effective lobbyists are often able to attract a disproportionate amount of attention from politicians. This has created a climate in which funding the most vocal organizations has become the norm. A better approach would be for governments to target specific social challenges and partner with CBNPs that have institutional capacity and expertise to design innovative, data-driven solutions to gradually eradicate each specific challenge.

Is protesting the most effective tool?

Many community groups believe that protesting is an important method of advocacy. Some community organizations spend a considerable amount of energy engaging in public demonstrations to highlight their cause. Other community organizations exist only for the purpose of advocacy and do very little besides host meetings, organize marches, and issue manifestos and petitions. When umbrella groups are established to advocate for a collection of community-based organizations, there is a tendency to spend an inordinate amount of time talking and consensus building. Governments, foundations, and charity consolidators will often fund conferences, studies, and permanent consultative forums. These can be used effectively by politicians to diffuse a crisis and to buy a bit of time. Organizing a meeting is a great tactic for ensuring that community activists feel as if they have been consulted. As important as these meetings sometimes seem, they often do not accomplish a great deal, and everyone goes back to their day-to-day reality and continues to do what they have always done. Not only that, the realities on the front lines are always evolving. A consultative meeting held in January will produce recommendations that are often irrelevant by the time June rolls around. To be balanced and fair, there is a need for advocacy. It is quite important to speak up and identify potential solutions to address what isn't working. The challenge is to combine advocacy with initiatives and actions that produce better outcomes.

Is there a need for more studies?

Studies are terrific and can help us develop a broader or deeper understanding of a particular issue. Some studies help illuminate areas that are easily misinterpreted. The challenge with most studies is that they take a fair amount of time to complete and are often more helpful in identifying historical trends than in identifying current realities. The situation on the ground changes rapidly. In today's reality, real-time, verifiable data is more helpful than a study that was completed a year ago.

> Real-time data coupled with qualitative information allows organizations to monitor a situation and gauge emerging trends as they unfold.

As an example, had a study of the food security situation in the city of Montreal been undertaken in 2015, the researchers would not have been able to foresee the influx of asylum seekers who arrived in 2017 and 2018. At the Mission where I serve, the number of asylum seekers who needed food assistance increased from 630 to more than 6500 from 2016 to 2018. There was no way to anticipate this change ahead of 2016, no matter how many studies might have been commissioned. A food security study in 2015 would not have been able to anticipate a surge in the movement of people from places like Nigeria, Syria, Venezuela, and Haiti, nor would it have been able to develop a rubric to formulate a response. No study could have accurately anticipated emerging needs in communities on the southern border of the United States. Yet in 2016, this massive increase in asylum seekers completely altered the profile of those in need in a number of Canadian and American cities. The real needs in a community often change suddenly.

Studies about social problems are informative, and they are often helpful in a macro sense, but they are unable to predict what will happen next in a world full of uncertainties. Real-time data coupled with qualitative information allows organizations to monitor a situation and gauge emerging trends as they unfold. The business world is experiencing a revolution due, in part, to rapid technological change that includes an acceleration of the availability of data. This change has not yet penetrated the non-profit world. Some would suggest that it is not even on the radar of many CBNPs. In the recent past, it was possible to rely on the conclusions of a study that took two years to complete, a year to review, and another few months to disseminate. In the 21st century, nobody can construct policies around studies that are three to five years old. The realities of challenges like poverty, homelessness, hunger, discrimination, and social exclusion are evolving, and the needs of real people are changing at a pace that is commensurate with the pace of change in the business world.

Are we prepared to frame issues differently?

My hope is that the thoughts in the next few chapters may help develop a new perspective on how we should go about addressing complex social challenges. There is little doubt that complex social challenges will exist in the near-term. Our North American economic system dictates that there will be disparity. In fact, every economic system that has been tried so far in the history of humanity has produced some level of disparity of wealth. There will also be disparity arising from individual physical, intellectual, or emotional limitations. Some people benefit from a more advantageous position in society. In some cases, this advantage was achieved by a combination of hard work and good fortune. A few people get a head start in life. They might enjoy the luxury of being handed opportunities like a superior education or relative economic prosperity. They may have also enjoyed social stability in their formative years. Others do not enjoy these kinds of benefits. Beyond that, when someone is forced to leave their country, they may have to deal with other significant disparities. An immigrant usually starts with inherent social and economic disadvantages. One of the current global realities is that displacement and mass migration is generating the largest movement of people since the Second World War. Significant demographic shifts are changing some of the realities of the United States and Canada. Societal norms are also shifting, which is causing political ripples that are raising new social issues related to inclusion.

In the past 25 years, the world has experienced the most profound level of technological and social change in history, and it is continuing to move at an unprecedented pace. It is unwise to propose that community-based non-profits ought to remain anchored in the same practices. Organizations that deliver services to vulnerable members of society must ensure that they constantly update their operations to align them with leading-edge thinking. They should be seeking out new ideas and testing new ways of doing things that are based on the latest science and the experience of other leading organizations. They cannot rely on what they once believed to be true. They cannot do what they have always done. They can't just affirm their intention to pursue "good work." They cannot brush only the surface of the problem. They must become much less activity-based and much more solution-oriented.

Virtually no community-based non-profit organization likes to admit that they may be metaphorically stuck in the mud. Yet every community-based non-profit organization needs to take a hard look in the mirror. The process of looking in the mirror may lead to discoveries that will be surprising. CBNPs may see some things that they don't like. Is it truly possible that, in the course of the history of trying to do good work, the good work may have helped fuel the problems they are trying to address? The passion for social change that is fundamental in a CBNP may be misguided, not because it has misidentified the problem, but because it has inadvertently misidentified the strategies and tactics that are necessary to address the cause of the problem.

> Organizations that deliver services to vulnerable members of society must ensure that they update their operations to align them with leading-edge thinking.

One of the major discoveries in the course of the 20th century was the potential to engineer quality into manufacturing processes rather than spend inordinate amounts of effort addressing quality failures after the manufacturing of a product had been completed. The same concept works for the CBNP sector. Can CBNPs move from a mindset of crisis management towards a mindset of crisis prevention?

A very practical example is the issue of the trajectory of young people who exit youth protection. Could a system be established that anticipates the needs of these young people? Can youth homelessness within this group be prevented rather than addressed once it happens? Would it save both money and lives? Another example is the network of day centres and overnight shelters that are largely assumed to be doing work that is good and important. Are they helpful if they merely act as a "respite centre" rather than as a catalyst for change? However, questions are being asked by leading organizations that call into question the operating model that underpins the shelter system and that drives the public funding of many of these iconic service providers. Is it helpful, in the long run, for a human being who has no fixed address to sleep in a shelter, be obliged to leave in the morning, wander around the city, drop in at a day centre, and return each evening to a place where a free meal and a free bed is available? Is it really a good idea to reinforce a welfare system that, in many cases, discourages people experiencing homelessness to make the effort to return to housing? After all, a person who subsists on a monthly government cheque is not going to conclude that spending most of it on housing is a wise move if it is easier to circulate in a network of well-meaning free overnight shelters and food providers. Furthermore, the current charitable system is either driven by program funding from government agencies or the generosity of donors who sincerely believe that they are helping change lives. Government funding tends to be attached to programs that nobody has any incentive to alter, even if they are ineffective at producing real change. Meanwhile, donors continue to give because they believe that they are doing the right thing or because they simply want to support efforts that they perceive as solutions because they reduce the visibility of the problem.

However, the question that all of us need to ask is: Can we do better than this? Somebody once wrote that: "Nothing is as painful as staying stuck somewhere you don't belong." Any organization that claims to be a service provider to the disadvantaged or the vulnerable has to be certain that it is positioned exactly where it ought to be, doing the right things in an effective manner, and progressing measurably towards the objectives that it claims to be pursuing. Furthermore, governments and members of the public who claim to support causes like housing, equality, education, and inclusion need to do so in a way that helps rather than hinders the cause.

1. https://www.bls.gov/opub/ted/2018/nonprofits-account-for-12-3-million-jobs-10-2-percent-of-private-sector-employment-in-2016.htm

2. https://grantspace.org/resources/knowledge-base/number-of-nonprofits-in-the-u-s/

3. https://www.thesunmagazine.org/issues/519/filling-the-void

4. https://nff.org/learn/survey

5. https://www.sac-isc.gc.ca/eng/1541187352297/1541187392851

CHAPTER 2
Can an "ah-ha moment" change your life?

A defining moment takes a long time to get over, if you ever do.
—Mick Jones

Travel is fatal to prejudice, bigotry, and narrow-mindedness…broad, wholesome, charitable views cannot be acquired by vegetating in one little corner of the earth all one's lifetime.
—Mark Twain

Everyone has a story. Our stories shape us. We all have a unique set of experiences that contribute to who we are. Our stories often help explain the various "why" factors in our lives. Why do we think the way we think? Why do we see things from a particular perspective? These include the reasons for many of our choices or explanations for how we understand ourselves and the world around us.

 Our stories help explain the various "why" factors in our lives.

I've been asked frequently how my career path led me to work in a community based non-profit setting. This seems to be of particular interest to young people who are seeking to do work that they believe to be meaningful. Almost any work can be meaningful and filled with purpose, however, it is vital that each person determine what they define as meaningful. It can be called "finding your purpose." Everyone ought to identify specific challenges that they feel compelled to tackle or initiatives that resonate with them. This can be building a business, designing structures, or being the best caregiver for children. It can be described as the development of a personal passion that can range from environmentally sustainable travel to stamp collecting, rock climbing, or rescuing abused animals. A person's passion is usually abundantly evident because they talk about what they care deeply about at every available opportunity. A purpose isn't always connected with a social challenge. It doesn't always lead to volunteering one's time to build houses for the poor or serving people at a palliative care centre. But sometimes it does!

27

My life plan did not include working at a community-based non-profit organization. I knew enough to realize that working in a community-based non-profit does not feel fulfilling and meaningful all the time.

> A person's passion is usually abundantly evident because they talk about what they care deeply about at every opportunity.

My complete personal journey could be the subject of another book. Some might consider it a moderately interesting story, but it is far from impressive or spectacular. I was the eldest of seven children in a relatively poor working-class family. My father suffered from narcolepsy that was so debilitating that he could literally "fall asleep" anywhere and at any time, unless he was doing active manual labour. As a result of this condition, and the loss of his parents at a very young age, he never completed high school. He worked for CN Railways inspecting freight cars from the age of 16 until the day he died at age 51. As the eldest child, I was often responsible for ensuring that my dad was kept clear of danger when he collapsed into brief periods of unconsciousness. It was always very embarrassing to have to wake him up from a deep sleep in front of strangers who often developed incorrect and uncharitable conclusions around what was happening. A narcoleptic appears to be intoxicated and disoriented when they awaken. I have vivid memories of feeling very self-conscious about having to shake my dad vigorously while we were riding home on the city bus so that we would not miss our stop. I learned years later that "narcoleptic sleep" often includes nightmares, which explained why he often woke up in a state of agitation.

My mother was a very intelligent, reasonably well-educated lady who was born and raised on a farm in Southwestern Ontario. She was the family's financial manager and provided our organizational backbone. She gave birth to seven children in a period of eleven years, and none were twins! Sadly, she was diagnosed with an aggressive form of breast cancer at age 37 and passed away when she was only 43.

Our family didn't have a lot of "things," but we did have a roof over our heads, and we were always well fed. We also knew that we were loved. Somewhat unusually, because our family was neither wealthy nor extremely poor, we alternated between two distinct socio-economic realities. In our neighbourhood and at school, we were considered to be on the wealthy end of the continuum because we lived in a large single-family house and we had a car. Most of my school friends lived in apartments or duplexes, many of which were somewhat rundown. Very few of our school friends' parents had cars. Many of my school friends saw us as the rich kids and thought that where we lived was upscale and desirable. The truth was that our house, while adequate, was in bad need of TLC and was held together by creative patchwork. On the other hand, in our other social circle—at church—we were exposed to a more solidly middle-class crowd. This group was composed of upwardly mobile people, many of whom made sure that we understood that they were higher on the food chain than we were. It became obvious to me that, even in a church setting, class-consciousness was ever-present.

Well-meaning individuals can inadvertently say the wrong thing at the wrong time. On the other hand, people who delight in exhibiting their class-consciousness are capable of saying some profoundly insensitive things without a modicum of self-awareness. This is particularly true for those who see themselves as having a slightly superior social rank. I will not easily forget overhearing a woman from our church explaining to her friends, "We all get along well because we are in the same social class, except for the Watts family." The woman had no idea that I heard what she said. Hearing it said aloud was not particularly traumatic. It was more like the discovery that one makes when someone turns on the overhead lights in a dimly lit room. It becomes possible to see things that you knew were there but hadn't really examined in detail. The woman was deeply class-conscious, but she was correct; our family was not in the same league.

The perception that we were outliers forged my intense determination to succeed. I had been exposed to people who had nicer homes, nicer cars, and more stuff. I decided that I did not want to be poor or appear to be uneducated. I threw myself into learning about the world around me, and I developed an interest in history and geography. Blessed with a good memory for random bits of information and a thirst for general knowledge, I managed to read everything that could be found, and I consumed every bit of available information. I even read every single page of a 24-volume set of encyclopedias before I reached the age of 11—something my siblings still tease me about.

I was also bitten by the entrepreneurial bug at an early age and became more or less economically self-sufficient in my early teens. I delivered newspapers, cleaned buildings, and took on various neighbourhood chores. I was pulling in $50 to $75 a week, which was big money at that time. I began to purchase my own clothing and even had my own personal supply of specific foods that my mother considered too costly to purchase for the entire family. This included maintaining a private cache of 2% milk, while the rest of the family had to drink powdered skim milk.

Several family crises ensued, including the tragic death of one of my brothers at age 11 and the premature death of my mother. I elected to forego a university education and decided that staying at home and supporting the family temporarily was the right thing to do. I never did attend university, something I deeply regret to this day. My sister assumed the role of den mother, and she has largely continued to be the family anchor, particularly after the passing of our father seven years after my mother left us.

When I was 24, I was hired in an entry-level sales role at one of Canada's largest manufacturing companies and was fortunate to be in the right place at the right time, career-wise, on quite a few occasions. This was the late 1980's, and the organization offered me a golden opportunity to succeed. It was an era when technology was beginning to transform the traditional business community. In that context, I enjoyed being coached by some incredible business mentors who encouraged and challenged me. By the age of 31, I had become the business leader of one of the most successful start-up divisions of the corporation. It was a small, entrepreneurial business that operated within a relatively obscure division of the company. The corporation had annual revenues of over one billion dollars, but the division I led quickly grew from less than a million dollars to over 20 million dollars of sales while commercializing new and innovative technologies. We built strong supply chain relationships and downstream partnerships before it was fashionable to do so. We functioned much like any under-capitalized start-up, but we were able to leverage the talents of a very dynamic core team. Our success and substantial profitability garnered a lot of attention within the corporation. This experience taught me about the power of building partnerships to advance an effort that would benefit multiple stakeholders. It also taught me that small, well-aligned teams could produce unbelievable outcomes. After a three-year interlude working for one of my best customers as VP of Sales and Marketing, I decided to begin my own consulting firm that specialized in accelerating team performance in complex environments. From 2001 to 2016, my consulting work provided me with the opportunity to travel and work in over eight different countries. It was a privilege to work on diverse assignments with large pharmaceutical companies, banks, retailers, government departments, and a variety of non-profits. These consulting assignments typically lasted for several months at a time and involved working with organizations to develop action plans to launch new products or services, and to work out issues that inevitably arose as they implemented the plans we had formulated together. In the case of one client, I had the distinct privilege of working alongside several internal teams and many of their downstream clients for more than nine years.

Travel was a constant reality. I logged 70 to 80 flight segments a year between 2001 and 2015 and collected plenty of frequent flyer miles. When she was a toddler, our youngest daughter used to wave at airplanes she saw in the sky, and say, "Hi Daddy!" My travel experiences were often mundane. Other times they were frustrating. Anyone who travels has stories about flight delays, bad hotels, or hair-raising cab rides. There were plenty of those experiences. There were other experiences that taught me lessons that would never have been learned had I stayed in an office. I learned to be observant, listen, watch how people communicate, and notice how they act and react. Inevitably, I saw things that provided me with fascinating stories that could be told in keynote talks or used to illustrate a couple of points when I was facilitating a strategic planning meeting. The stories and experiences often illuminated the value of wise leadership, innovation, or customer centric behaviour.

> I learned to be observant, listen, watch how people communicate, and notice how they act and react.

Experiences and stories are one thing, but a moment of clarity that hits like a bolt of lightning is something altogether different. Sometimes they are called "ah-ha moments." I can identify several "ah-ha moments" in my life. They seem to happen when they are least expected. The one I describe in the pages that follow happened when I was about as far away from home as I could be. Sometimes, you have to be a long way from your home to be in a position to see and appreciate something you have never grasped before. Sometimes, if you pay attention, it can be life altering.

An "Ah-Ha Moment" Story

I was invited to do some business presentations in Cape Town, South Africa in May of 2007. I had the privilege of meeting some wonderful people and having great discussions about South Africa and the changes that were taking place in that country. When we were free, I had the opportunity to travel with my hosts to see wineries near Stellenbosch and enjoy the incredible scenery. On my final day in the country, there were no formal business meetings scheduled. I decided to stroll down to the waterfront area of Cape Town. One of the options I had considered was a trip out to Robben Island. Thinking that it was something I might never again get a chance to experience, I bought a ticket. The input I had received from my hosts was that Robben Island wasn't worth the price and that the crossing was a bit rough. They were correct about the crossing. They were dead wrong about the value of the visit.

Upon disembarking on the island, our group was met by a guide and given a brief bus tour. Robben Island, home of the prison that was used in the apartheid era as a preferred location for the incarceration of political prisoners, had also been used in earlier days as a whaling station, a leper colony, and a Second World War defense outpost. In 1997, it was designated as a UN World Heritage Site. It is described as a unique symbol to "the triumph of the human spirit over adversity, suffering, and injustice."

The bus stopped at a non-descript quarry, and our tour guide invited us to disembark and stand around a small pile of stones. He was a friendly man in a dark leather jacket who introduced himself using his number—not his name. We learned that many of the tour guides were former prisoners of Robben Island. A prisoner's number was his identification. He explained that the quarry was the place where prisoners were forced to work during their time on the island. He told us that the small pile of stones was symbolic, but because of the tours that came to the island, it was fast becoming the most photographed pile of rocks in the world. Naturally, I took a picture!

He walked us around the prison complex, describing the various routines of prison life. We had the opportunity to see the cell of prisoner number 46664, the most famous prisoner, Nelson Mandela. It is not much larger than a closet.

At one point, our tour guide stopped and asked us each where we were from. He acknowledged the people from various countries in the world, often by saying something positive about that country. The last two people to identify themselves were a woman from Great Britain and me. He was strangely cold towards the woman from Great Britain, acting almost as if he had no use for that country. When I identified myself as a Canadian, he walked directly towards me, looked me squarely in the eye, shook my hand, and in a loud and clear voice said, "I want to thank you for your government's support and your solidarity with South Africa during our struggle against the evils of apartheid." His statement made me wonder if his chilly reaction to the woman from Great Britain was due to that country's hesitancy to condemn the South African regime in the 1980's when Margaret Thatcher waffled on imposing sanctions, despite the existence of a broad international consensus that no effort should be spared to isolate the country economically.

He then asked us if we had any questions for him. Coincidentally, the only question came from the woman from Great Britain. She asked, "As a former prisoner, do you find it at all disturbing that you are back here as a tour guide, and do you find that the place haunts you just a bit?" *A fair question,* I thought.

Our tour guide stiffened visibly, and he pulled at the lapels of his leather jacket. He looked extremely serious, almost as if the question had offended him. Frankly, I thought he was going to give the woman a piece of his mind. I was imagining him saying something like: "Maybe you don't fully appreciate how wrong apartheid was, and maybe you don't understand that people like me need to show up here every day to educate ignorant people like you." However, he did not respond with any sign of anger or annoyance. What he said to her contributed in a big way to my "ah-ha moment".

He walked slowly towards her and said, "Madam, I am so glad you asked that question." He placed real emphasis on the word "so," and he paused for emphasis, delivering the rest of his answer slowly and deliberately. "Far from being haunted by this place, I am an essential witness in this place. You see, Madam, the enemy is not the people who put my comrades and me in this prison. The enemy is the kind of thinking that caused a place like this to exist. The enemy is evil and intolerance wherever it is. Look around in our world. Wherever there is violence and discrimination, there is also the absence of humanity. Robben Island is a UN World Heritage Site that highlights the need for understanding and tolerance in the face of injustice and inhumanity."

He paused and looked around at us. "Have any of you ever heard of the 'R' word?" He asked the question with such gusto that nobody responded. He continued, "Here in South Africa, we had a commission that held hearings about evil things that were done in the apartheid era. People appeared in front of the commission and told the truth about things they did. The truth was sometimes hard to tell and even harder to hear. However, with truth came the possibility of forgiveness and even reconciliation. Yes, the 'R' word is reconciliation. And this country, indeed, most of the world needs reconciliation." He placed particular emphasis on the word reconciliation every time he used it.

Then he delivered the conclusion to his answer. Turning back to the woman from Great Britain he said, "Madam, the 'R' word, reconciliation, can be just another word. This island, this jail, stands as a beacon to the world of the reality that injustice and evil exist, but it holds high the value of reconciliation. And I want to live in a place where the 'R' word is more than a word, where it is a reality." Then he stepped back, took a deep breath, and said, "So you see, ladies and gentlemen, I must be here. If I believe in reconciliation, I must be part of the process that helps my country move towards the reality of reconciliation." There were no further questions.

So, what was the "ah-ha moment?" What changed? For the next few hours, I was simply overwhelmed, and after returning to the mainland, I went to a restaurant for lunch and wrote down what had just happened. Then I began to see the genius in his response.

Here was a man who had every right to be bitter. It would not have been terribly unusual for him to be actively looking for a way to deliver a bit of payback to a group of people who had treated him badly. In his case, he told us that he spent four years on Robben Island. When Nelson Mandela was released from prison in 1990, it led to an agreement that eventually ushered in majority rule in South Africa. After lengthy negotiations, Mandela became the country's first black President in May 1994. So was it time for revenge? Most people are aware that Nelson Mandela worked tirelessly to unite the country and prevent widespread recrimination. Mr. Mandela's leadership was centred on developing the principles of reconciliation at every level of South African society, and the process was not instantaneous or easy. Our tour guide understood the theory. More importantly, he was intent on putting the theory into action in a way that contributed to the change he believed was essential for his country.

In reflecting on the answer to the question, the tour guide had identified four universal principles that are essential for anyone who wants to be part of an effort that will lead to a transformation in their communities. They are also principles that can be life changing at a personal level. These are simple but profound ideas that I uncovered in this "ah-ha moment".

1. **Be prepared to let go of any unnecessary baggage**
   Our tour guide had plenty of reason to be consumed by the desire for retribution. At the very least, he could have invested time seeking out the former guards from Robben Island and exacting revenge. After all, he had been jailed by a regime that was judged by most of the world to be evil and illegitimate. The guards were the undisputed masters of the island and had a mandate to punish the prisoners and keep them in line. Despite his experience of mistreatment, he consciously recognized that responding with anger or hatred was both unhelpful and unhealthy.

Letting go of baggage does not mean abandoning the pursuit of justice.

Far too many of us spend far too much of our time wallowing in past issues or plotting revenge for perceived slights. We haul around baggage that we do not need to carry. Letting go of baggage does not mean abandoning the pursuit of justice. Nobody ought to bury serious issues like abuse, psychological trauma, or the experience of violence. These usually require years of professional counselling to address. The challenge that many of us wrestle with is that we refuse to put aside petty issues, differences of opinion, or miscommunication. We allow unimportant things to linger and fester. We often hold grudges based on perceptions. Some of us allow bitterness to build and inform how we act. Ultimately, if we want to be the kind of people who can help transform our world, we must face up to resentments and slights we are harbouring. We need to stop clinging to our unnecessary baggage.

2. **Be crystal clear on the cause**

   Our tour guide knew exactly what the cause was. He knew what was important and what did not matter. The purpose of his life and work was to ensure that the "R" word was more than a word that people would use without any meaning.

   In my case, I always felt that my cause was to help people and organizations achieve their full potential. It was the unique value proposition of my consulting practice. I invested thousands of hours working with teams and leaders to help them understand and appreciate the differences in their communication styles and to develop their teams in ways that would produce results. However, what I heard on Robben Island put a bug in my ear that eventually turned into a personal and professional sense of discontent. Was I clear enough in my own mind about my cause? If an opportunity presented itself, would I be prepared to take it if it were more closely aligned with how I articulated my cause?

3. **Refuse to settle**

   The tour guide who led us around the prison could have decided that he had done enough. After all, he had gone to prison. He had been incarcerated while fighting for justice and equality. Sure, the country had emerged from the apartheid era and was beginning to transform itself. Nonetheless, he did not feel that his mission was complete. Instead, he was determined to actively participate in an unusual experiment—an African experiment that had not been undertaken with any success anywhere else on the continent. It did (and still does) require its participants to refuse to settle for the responses of the past and seek out new answers, new pathways, and new solutions.

   My professional experience trained me to refuse to accept standard answers when faced with challenges. In my early thirties, I had been given the opportunity to manage a small business inside a big corporation at a time when we were able to create a market that had not previously existed. This was a fun ride. When I decided to jump into the business of being a consultant, I advised clients about avoiding the trap of failing to validate their underlying business assumptions. We frequently re-framed issues together, reimagined alternatives, and re-invented concepts in order to avoid repeating past errors or to avoid stagnation. Nonetheless, the more I reflected on what I heard from our tour guide, the more I wondered if I had inadvertently begun to settle. Was there a more important calling? Most human beings are prepared to settle for the status quo when there is no sense of discomfort, no burning platform. Had I, in my mid-forties begun to settle? Was there more that needed to be done?

> Most human beings are prepared to settle for the status quo when there is no sense of discomfort, no burning platform.

4. **Engage others in the solution**

    The tour guide could not achieve reconciliation in South Africa all alone. It was going to take the efforts of all South Africans. Nelson Mandela set the tone by the way that he behaved, both before and after being elected President of the country. His leadership made a difference, but the point the tour guide made was that we all have a part to play. It may seem like a small part, but it is a vital part. Our tour guide, by conducting tours around Robben Island and engaging visitors from all over the world in the course of his day-to-day work, was spreading the message of reconciliation far beyond the borders of his country.

> Nothing much happens in an organization without a team effort.

    Long before my trip to South Africa it had become clear to me that valiant individual efforts were commendable but team alignment was a force multiplier. Nothing much happens in an organization without a team effort. Individual efforts are important, but the actions of individuals produce exponentially better outcomes when they are supported by a fully engaged team. The same is true in a community; significant progress usually happens via a social movement. Leaders are essential to set the tone, but observable change rarely happens because of a single inspirational speech by a leader or a podium-pounding declaration by an elected official. Real change comes about when perceptions around an issue change, galvanizing the public. In South Africa, I observed both individual commitment to a new way of thinking and a broader alignment that came from leadership that invited people to join in a process of reconciliation.

Change can be incremental, or it can gather steam and explode suddenly. An example of this kind of rapid change is the approach to talking about mental illness in 2020, as compared to the stigma and the silence that existed a few short decades ago. What happened? We all became better informed because people and organizations in the medical, business, and entertainment sectors elected to proactively engage the public's consciousness and re-position the reality of the condition, rather than accept the typical narrative or the painful silence that had been the norm for decades.

I returned home from South Africa with an evolving sense of purpose. While the "ah-ha moment" was very real, the process of turning the moment into meaningful action on my part was probably a lot slower than it should have been. Perhaps I wasn't quite prepared for what I might have to give up in order to pursue a cause that mattered.

> What cause could be more important than serving the people who serve the disadvantaged and vulnerable people in the city where I live?

Ultimately, when the unexpected opportunity of serving at a local CBNP presented itself, I had arrived at a point where I was ready to embrace it. I did not plan to take on the role of leading the organization where I currently serve. The "Robben Island moment" came flooding back. What cause could be more important than serving the people who serve the disadvantaged and vulnerable people in the city where I live?

Why does any of this matter? Each one of us will likely experience an "ah-ha moment" at some point in our lives. Most people will eventually come face-to-face with something that shifts his or her assessment of what is important. These moments can produce clarity. Many of us have faced specific and memorable points of adversity. Some will simply try to get through these tests rather than reflect on them. Others emerge from personal reversals or tragic events and use them as a springboard to accomplish great things. Sadly, there are also people who endure difficulties and do not learn a single thing from them. For those who are able to recognize opportunity in the face of a reversal, or find moments of clarity during periods of adversity, any challenge can become a catalyst for growth. We have all heard inspirational stories of people who would say that their worst tragedy prepared them to tackle a cause for which they had been born.

CHAPTER 3
Who is my neighbour?

Charities…operate by skimming the surface of very deep problems without comparable depth in their solution, and sometimes even exacerbate the problem.
—Cate MacDonald

Giving is not just about making a donation. It is about making a difference.
—Kathy Calvin

THE PROBLEM: We have to recognize that helping isn't enough. When we help, we should ensure that our help isn't just an act of kindness, but rather an action that is designed to ensure a continuum of care that leads to a permanent solution.

The ABC's of charity

If everyone understands basic charitable principles, why waste time on an entire chapter to discuss them? The reason is that most people believe that they know about them, but they may not have taken the time to fully understand them. Most will recognize that awareness does not always generate deeper understanding, and deeper understanding does not always lead to action. A person can be aware of something but not understand it. Additionally, gaining understanding doesn't guarantee that the next step is the right step.

Charity, by definition, is the giving of help, typically in the form of money, to those in need. On the surface this seems like a simple definition. If anyone sees someone in need and provides them with assistance or money, we usually conclude that this type of response constitutes charity. But how does one define need? How can any reasonable person ascertain the legitimacy of need? How can someone know that the best thing to do in a specific situation is to provide spontaneous help or money? What can be done if someone who is clearly in need refuses to accept all offers of assistance?

Charity, to a critic of charity, is nothing more than a "handout." For the sceptical person accosted by a beggar or panhandler, giving money is a throw-away gesture—given out of pure sympathy or as a function of guilt. After all, who hasn't been "guilted" into making a donation? The adorable kid asks us to buy a chocolate bar for her school's fundraiser.

We buy the chocolate bar, not because we need it, but because we feel we have to. It may be possible to recall an experience of being with a group of colleagues in a restaurant when a stranger approaches the table and puts a card in front of one of the members of the dining party. The card indicates that the person who approached the group is deaf or disabled and includes a request for a financial contribution. Everyone may have, reluctantly, agreed to donate a few dollars. Guilt can work as a cash generator, but it does not engage people in a well-defined purpose.

A significant number of people in North America believe that social challenges are enabled and facilitated by charitable handouts. There is a percentage of the population who believe that giving to those in need results in an encouragement of a lifestyle of extracting from the system. A great deal of research has been conducted on the benefits and limits of charitable activities, particularly as they relate to those in the developing world. This has become a subject of considerable debate that has extended into an investigation of the relative effectiveness of charitable activity in places like the United States of America and Canada. The main interest of this research has been to attempt to uncover whether a case can be made for the predictability of outcomes linked to specific charitable endeavours.

Still, the power of human emotions like empathy and the desire to help are fundamental to who we are. If someone is truly in need and we see the need, the gut level response should be to want to help. Many people instinctively feel like they should provide something to a person in need. Very few of us feel good about walking away from a hungry person. Recently, we left a local restaurant and one of my family members, having failed to completely finish a rather large steak, was carrying a container with the leftovers. She spotted a man who was begging and asked him if he was hungry. When he said he was, she gave him the container. She felt like his immediate need was more important than retaining the piece of steak. Charity is about developing the ability to see need and respond instinctively to need. The challenge is that nobody can see every need or care for everybody. If someone is a volunteer or a full-time employee in an organization that can reach thousands of disadvantaged people, the challenge is entirely similar. There is always a limit. The need is always greater than the resources that are immediately available to respond to the need.

> The challenge is that nobody can see every need or care for everybody.

Community-based non-profit organizations that provide relief to those in difficulty are limited by money, geography, and scope of operations. A generous donor can't hope to address every need that exists, even if the donor has millions of dollars to give away. Even philanthropists like Bill Gates or Warren Buffet have limited resources.

Those of us who have visited a developing country, where begging is a way of life and poverty is endemic, will have had the experience of feeling overwhelmed, even if it was possible to deliberately look in the other direction. It is tough to come to grips with the reality of having a limited capacity to respond. When a tourist is surrounded by kids clamouring for a donation on the street, it is hard to look them in the eye and walk away. It is even harder to give to one person and ignore others. The challenge is to know where to begin. Is it better to give a little bit of money to a lot of people, or pick one person and give a significant amount? Who is the neediest of the needy? Where does one draw the line? Are they really needy or is this a scam? Are we enabling a lifestyle of dependency if we give? Is any amount of money really going to help the person or their family?

A Story About the Challenges of Charitable Reflexes

> I was walking in the downtown core of Montreal and a man approached me with the stage presence of a well-rehearsed actor. He greeted me with the swagger and exaggerated confidence of a carnival barker. He launched right into his narrative. His story was well constructed, but he had stumbled on the wrong person to share it with!
>
> He explained that he was from out of town and had planned to take the bus back to his home, but he had lost his bus ticket. This was forcing him to stay in local emergency shelters. He named several of them. So far, so good, although the lost bus ticket story is used with regularity by proficient panhandlers. It works on the public because many people find it plausible. The aim is to get the potential sympathetic donor to invest a bit of time listening to the story. The details matter, but there is room for a bit of dramatic embellishment. Next, the storyteller will evaluate the level of sympathy he has generated and make a monetary request based on the capacity he attributes to the potential donor. This man did a fine job on the front end. As he concluded his tale of a journey gone wrong, he indicated that he needed ten dollars to pay for his night's lodging at a specific shelter, which he named. He then offered the additional information that Welcome Hall Mission was full. Minor tactical error!
>
> I pulled out one of my business cards and suggested that he did not have his story straight. In fact, the emergency shelter that he said he wanted

> to reach did not charge ten dollars per night. I added that the shelter in question had filled up at two o'clock that day, and that if he took my card and walked down the hill, and then three blocks west, he would be able to use my business card to obtain a bed for the night. Our shelter was not full. How did I know? I asked him to read the title on my business card. He looked at it, pocketed it, and immediately decided that I was not his ideal funding prospect. As I walked away, I observed that he had quickly moved on to tell the same story to another individual on the street. With his talent for engagement and his interesting pitch, he might have been able to accumulate several hundred dollars that evening.

Some people who find themselves in real difficulty will resort to the indignities of street begging. There are legitimate stories of tragic circumstances and travel gone wrong. It is usually difficult to assess the legitimacy of a story presented to us by a person who claims to be in a dire situation. It isn't wrong to feel sympathy for someone, nor is it necessarily inappropriate to respond to a perceived need. Should we give money? Should we buy a coffee or food? What is the best way to help? These are all valid questions that are best addressed by taking a few steps back and considering three important elements.

Do I have a clear understanding of the problem?

Am I equipped to respond appropriately to the person or the problem?

Will the action that I am contemplating put an end to the problem or will it simply provide temporary relief that does little to resolve a specific predicament?

There are some situations in which it is important to act to provide immediate care or to save a life, even if we are ill-prepared, untrained and under-equipped. However, there is an equal need to ensure that we don't cultivate a reflex to respond to situations unwisely or inappropriately. In the end, most of us are usually forced to trust our common sense to respond to a perceived immediate need.

How can a response be the correct response if we rely on assumptions rather than facts?

One of the challenges for most CBNPs is to develop a clear case that demonstrates that specific actions lead to specific outcomes. Demonstrating cause and effect in a very complex and evolving environment is not an easy thing to do. There is an assumption that charitable work, particularly in a community-based non-profit organization, is messy and necessarily disorganized. That leads people to accept that there is a certain level of randomness to the activities of the organization. This comes from the understanding that human behaviour can be unpredictable and that non-profit organizations are dealing with human beings who are in crisis. This, in turn, means that most CBNPs will inevitably have to respond to realities that are inherently unpredictable.

There has been a historical tendency to assume that very few elements in the field of community work can be objectively evaluated. There has also been considerable resistance in the community-based non-profit sector to the collection and use of empirical measurements or relevant data. Many organizations, particularly those that focus on some of the more vulnerable people groups, will argue that data collection and analysis is too time-consuming and takes away from the time they can spend with their clients. Some do not have the resources to collect any verifiable data. Some make claims about potential privacy concerns, but they typically lack a complete understanding of the fundamental principles that surround privacy, as it relates to the management of personal data.

> There has been considerable resistance in the community-based non-profit sector to the collection and use of empirical measurements or relevant data.

There is no coherent reason why a CBNP can't collect and retain personal information, as long as they obey the law and follow the kinds of protocols that are typically employed by hospitals. Some organizations bristle at the idea of sharing information among service providers because they feel like they own client files. The reality is that any organization that collects and retains personal information is a mere caretaker of that personal information. The client owns their personal information, and the organization is expected to take reasonable steps to safeguard it. Therefore, a client can provide informed consent that allows an agency to collect and share relevant information with other agencies, provided the process adheres to privacy provisions within the legal framework of the state or province. The principal premise of selective data sharing is that it provides a client with better services by avoiding bureaucratic duplication.

Other CBNPs conclude that any emphasis on the collection of data leads towards a philosophy that dehumanizes human suffering by ignoring the struggles of real people. They believe that data will become more important than names and faces. There is a fear that statistical analysis will diminish the stories of those who suffer, and that an unacceptable individual reality will become lost inside a set of numbers or percentages. In addition, many CBNPs are utterly immersed in the challenge of providing services to those in need, and do not have the capability or the organizational disciplines in place to collect anything other than the most basic information about the people that they serve.

In making a case for effective systems that help CBNPs collect and evaluate relevant data, it is important to underline that this does not mean anyone should be turning tragic stories into data points. Individual tragedies and compelling stories are extremely important, but they cannot be credibly positioned as representative of a bigger issue without clear evidence. Most community-based non-profit groups are typically trying to address community needs, not merely respond to random individual cases of need. Actions to address the broad ensemble of social problems cannot be undertaken simply by assembling a collection of real-life stories of struggle, discrimination, social exclusion, or poverty. The stories matter. The people matter. One person who is disenfranchised is one too many. However, policies and funding cannot be driven or guided by anecdotes. They have to be supported by real-time data.

There is a real need in the sector for issues and problems to be quantified so that they can be properly evaluated. In round table discussions in the CBNP world, problems are frequently described using general words such as "lots," "big," "major," "considerable," "sizable," and "growing." There is a reluctance to provide a number rather than use a word like "lots." Does "lots" of people mean ten people or a hundred people? What constitutes a "growing" problem? If an organization indicates that there is a crisis due to a 40% increase in demand for its services, it makes a difference if the 40% increase refers to 20 people or 400 people.

> If an organization indicates that there is a crisis due to a 40% increase in demand for its services, it makes a difference if the 40% increase refers to 20 people or 400 people.

There are also numerous examples of the misuse of statistics or the promulgation of incomplete information that is designed to impress potential donors. An organization may gain considerable media attention by claiming that they have to turn 90 vulnerable women away from nightly shelter every month. This can lead politicians and the public to conclude that 90 women are unsheltered. However, if the organization cannot provide by-name data that corroborates their assertion, then it is unclear if they turned away 90 different women or if they turned away the same 3 women each night of the month. If a community-based non-profit organization refuses to employ practices that include verifiable measurement systems, then it is difficult to determine if there is a significant gap in the services needed. Nobody, including the CBNP, is in a position to objectively determine the scope of the problem.

Perhaps one of the big questions to ask is: Will an action or activity accomplish what it sets out to do? Organizations that provide aid internationally have begun to ask questions about the suitability of their activities. For example, does building a well in a village make that village permanently healthier and self-sustaining or does it completely alter the social dynamic in ways that are harmful? Does giving free shoes to people in Africa provide an essential service to needy folks or does it create chaos in the local economy?

In North American CBNPs, there has been a reluctance to entertain similar questions. Is handing a blanket to a person who is huddled in the corner of the street in Chicago an appropriate response so that she does not freeze, or does that act serve to simply encourage her to stay in an unacceptable place (on the street)? Does providing an under-resourced person with a bag of various non-perishable grocery items help them make it to the end of the month, or does it promote dependency and eating habits that centre on a diet of processed food that contributes to an unhealthy lifestyle? Does a drop-in centre for street-youth provide real help if it is only open on weekdays from noon until seven in the evening? What happens when the doors close for the evening and where do the clients go on weekends? Does supplying breakfasts to children in school respond in the best possible manner to the challenge faced by schools that welcome hungry children every morning, or does it promote a perception of inequality among highly impressionable youngsters who can point to those who get the free food and label them as "poor kids"? Some programs distribute food to every child in an effort to avoid the stigma that can be associated with receiving a "free" lunch. The question should be asked: Is that the best use of scarce resources?

A number of additional questions should also run through the minds of those who are inclined to respond to perceived needs. When contemplating a donation to a community-based non-profit organization it is entirely reasonable for a potential donor ought to ask a lot of questions to ensure that they understand what their donation will accomplish. This could include deeper questions about the strategy, approach, and tactical effectiveness of the effort being undertaken. Has the problem been framed correctly? Is the response advocated by the organization the best response? Is it based on best practices that have been documented? How is the problem changing or evolving? Is the not-profit organization simply doing good work and hoping for the best?

The story that guides the understanding of many charitable actions

To look at the typical North American approach to giving and to get a good grip on how perceptions of generosity may need to be reconsidered, it is helpful to examine one of the better-known (but least understood) narratives that form the basis for many of our charitable reflexes.

The story of the Good Samaritan is a reasonably well-known reference point in Western culture. Even if one does not subscribe to Judeo-Christian traditions or consider the parables of Jesus to be relevant to them, the term "Good Samaritan" is widely recognized in Western culture. The Good Samaritan narrative has developed into a well-understood metaphor when anyone speaks to the issue of helping the less fortunate. "Good Samaritan Laws" have been adopted in some jurisdictions to protect charitable behaviours. This is usually a legislative framework that provides some legal protection to people who give assistance to those who are injured, ill, in peril, or otherwise incapacitated.

In the highlighted section below, the narrative of the story includes a preamble to the traditional parable that many readers will not have seen or heard about. It is essential to the context of the principles of "Good Samaritanism" and, frankly, any 21st-century reference to being a "Good Samaritan" to include an understanding of the 1st-century context of the parable.

> *One day an expert in religious law stood up to test Jesus by asking him this question: "Teacher, what should I do to inherit eternal life?" Jesus replied, "What does the law of Moses say? How do you read it?" The man answered, "'You must love the Lord your God with all your heart, all your soul, all your strength, and all your mind,' and, 'Love your neighbour as yourself.'" "Right!" Jesus told him. "Do this and you will live!" The man wanted to justify his actions, so he asked Jesus, "And who is my neighbour?" Jesus responded with this parable.*
>
> *"A Jewish man was travelling from Jerusalem down to Jericho, and he was attacked by bandits. They stripped him of his clothes, beat him up, and left him half dead beside the road.*
>
> *"By chance, a priest came along. But when he saw the man lying there, he crossed to the other side of the road and passed him by. A Temple assistant walked over and looked at him lying there, but he also passed by on the other side.*

> *"Then a despised Samaritan came along, and when he saw the man, he felt compassion for him. Going over to him, the Samaritan soothed his wounds with olive oil and wine and bandaged them. Then he put the man on his own donkey and took him to an inn, where he took care of him. The next day he handed the innkeeper two silver coins, telling him, 'Take care of this man. If his bill runs higher than this, I'll pay you the next time I'm here.'*
>
> *"Now which of these three would you say was a neighbour to the man who was attacked by bandits?" Jesus asked. The man replied, "The one who showed him mercy." Then Jesus said, "Yes, now go and do the same."* 1
>
> Luke 10:30-36

The key takeaway points

On the surface, this is a well-narrated story that can force us to pause and evaluate our own responses. It causes a reader to wonder if they are more like one of the two people who failed to help the victim. It validates the actions taken by the "despised Samaritan" who went out of his way to provide extraordinary care. A surface-level analysis, while important, doesn't lead anyone to the real point of the story. When someone uses the term "Good Samaritan," they are usually referring to a kind act. However, being a "Good Samaritan," based on the framing of the story by the original storyteller, carries much more nuance than most people realize. Generally speaking, readers misunderstand the essence of the story for three reasons.

> Being a "Good Samaritan," based on the framing of the story by the original storyteller, carries much more nuance than most people realize.

1. **A reader may not be equipped to incorporate the context**
   The context of the story is critical. The context sets up the reason why the story was being told in the first place. In the preamble to the story, Jesus, the storyteller, is engaged in an important discussion with a legal expert. The issue that was raised was a hotly debated topic at the time. Was there such a thing as "eternal life" and, if so, how might a well-meaning, righteous Jewish man make sure that he obtained it, presuming he did his level best to obey all the laws and customs taught by the Rabbis. Employing an effective teaching method, Jesus responds to a question from the legal expert with an open-ended question of his own. Jesus did not offer

his view or opinion. Instead, he asked the legal expert to explain how he would personally interpret the Law of Moses. Jewish religious law was considered the basis for understanding all aspects of morality in that particular culture at that time. In essence, the challenge was one of interpretation.

Lawyers and people who study legal texts know that a key component of any legal document is a section that provides definitions. How one defines a word or a term matters a great deal. A definition can alter an interpretation. In this case, the discussion was framed to depend on the definition of the term "neighbour." The legal expert asks, "Who is my neighbour?" On the surface, this is a reasonable question. The historian who recorded the conversation adds his view suggesting that this legal expert was looking for an opinion that would justify his lifestyle. Legally, it was quite conceivable that a definition of the word "neighbour" might be open to debate. Could a neighbour be reasonably limited to a person who shared the same nationality, religious affiliation, or social class? Alternatively, did the word refer to a person living next door? What about a person who lived one street away? The inference was that if everyone had to love their neighbour as they loved themselves then, logically, there might be some non-neighbours that could reasonably be excluded from this requirement. After all, the commandment did not say, "Love *everyone* as yourself."

> An understanding of the word "neighbour" is a critical part of any debate around caring and responding to needs in the 21st century.

An understanding of the definition of the word "neighbour" is a critical part of any debate around caring and responding to needs in the 21st century. Are we responsible for the predicament of people in another city or in every faraway country? Do we have to do something about the hungry person who is in the downtown core of the city, if we live and work in the suburbs? Is it really a neighbourhood issue if it is utterly impractical or logistically challenging to address a problem that we may learn about? The people listening to the story may have been forced to re-think their preconceptions. Two thousand years later, the story continues to raise questions and suggest possible conclusions about how we should respond to needs in the world around us.

2. **A reader may be unaware of the cultural subtleties in the story**
It is important to recognize that the story itself was brilliantly crafted to ensure a certain amount of ambiguity. It contains a clear reference to the gender of the

unfortunate person who was robbed and left helpless at the side of the road. It is impossible to assume anything about the victim's social status, nationality, or religious affiliation. Furthermore, the man was obviously a traveller so we know that he was not in his neighbourhood. The robbed individual at the side of the road had no money, no belongings, and no clothing. These facts matter in the context of the culture of that time period because the way the story was told prevented the listener from developing a proposed action plan based on the social status of the victim. For example, had the injured person been extremely poor or extremely wealthy, this would have been evident by looking at his clothing. Without clothing or belongings as a reference point, the victim was presented in the abstract—just a nameless individual on the side of the road, without any indication of economic status.

Another cultural subtlety embedded in the story is the reason why the initial two travellers failed to provide assistance. A casual reader might assume that the storyteller wants us to believe that these two religious men were callous or uncaring. They may have been self-centered, but that is not the essence of the intended message. In the culture of the first century, priests and temple employees were required to maintain ritual purity. Rules and customs dictated many things, including what they were permitted to touch or handle. These rules had to be carefully observed. One rule was that they could not come into contact with a dead body or they would be required to undergo a comprehensive process of purification. This purification process was time-consuming, and it was the first century equivalent of being benched on a sports team. As a temple employee, they would have been ineligible to serve, and everyone in the tight-knit temple community would know about it. The fact that the victim is portrayed as "half dead" suggests that he might have appeared to be dead. This uncertainty presented a serious problem for the first two men on the scene.

The question became one of expediency in that moment of decision. In one sense, they could argue that they acted correctly by avoiding an unknown situation that could have caused them tremendous professional inconvenience. They may have been tempted to respond differently had this been a wealthy friend or a fellow employee of the temple. The easiest thing to do was to avoid getting involved. Such avoidance would have been completely understandable to a first-century audience. Unless a reader is well educated in the traditions of Jewish practices in that era, our 21st-century understanding may steer us towards an overly judgmental attitude towards the two religious characters in the story.

As hard as it may be for a modern reader to understand, the truth is that they had somewhat understandable reasons for doing what they did. Martin Luther King Junior, writing about this story, provided terrific insight by suggesting, "The first question the priest asked was, 'If I stop to help this man, what will happen to me?' But the Good Samaritan reversed the question: 'If I do not stop to help this man, what will happen to him?'"

3. **A reader may stop reading before the end of the story**

    If the story began with the words, "a Jewish man…" and it ended with an application of oil, wine, and bandages, the message would be an anecdote about on-the-spot kindness. This has caused many people to believe that being a modern day "Good Samaritan" means giving spontaneous, temporary relief to needy people. Handing out coffee, soup, or food to a hungry person, giving a blanket to someone sleeping in the subway, or tossing a few coins to a beggar might be equated to the actions of the Samaritan in the story.

    A serious student of the narrative simply cannot arrive at that kind of a conclusion from this story. One of the critical elements of the story is that the on-the-spot help provided was not where the narrative ended, nor is it the moral point of the story. The Samaritan did much more than merely ensure the momentary survival of the victim. He did not make a tax-deductible donation to an organization in Jericho that served the victims of robbery. He did not merely bandage him up, give him some food, and wish him pleasant future travels. He accompanied the victim away from danger, transported him to a safe place and made sure that ongoing care and lodging was made available. This is one of the most important messages that is being transmitted. It is not enough to help someone in a crisis. If we wish to be "Good Samaritans," we must respond appropriately to a person's immediate crisis and be willing to accompany them to a safer place. Someone who seeks to be helpful should ensure that ongoing care is provided and must be non-territorial, allowing other people to take over and provide the next phase of care. We cannot assume that we are always capable or qualified to provide a full continuum of care.

If we wish to be "Good Samaritans," we must respond appropriately to a person's immediate crisis and be willing to accompany them to a safer place.

Applying the core principles

To understand the major point of the story, it is essential to return to the question that caused the story to be told. The question was, "Who is my neighbour?" The answer is that our neighbour is whoever is in front of us. The response of the legal expert and the affirmation of the storyteller ought to lead a 21st century reader to conclude that "Good Samaritanism" means more than doing the right thing on the spot. It means more than showing unparalleled mercy. It means redefining the word "neighbour," and it means ensuring that there are corridors of referral and continuity of care for those in need. "Good Samaritanism" also includes an abandonment of prejudices and preconceptions. If someone wants to help the vulnerable, they will have to jettison their biases and perceptions. They might even need to step outside societal norms and the expectations of peers.

The principles of "Good Samaritanism" remain relevant in the context of the typical charitable reflexes of the 21st century. For some people, the message that resonates is a personal call to action. It suggests the need to be ready to respond to any compelling need that presents itself. This takeaway is important, but incomplete. First, it is important to ensure that any individual action can be part of a longer-term approach that ensures a continuum of care. Temporary "Band-Aids," while important, are never the solution to complex social issues. Second, a personal response may be very unwise if a person is not equipped to address the need. Sometimes the answer isn't to act ourselves, but to summon someone else who is qualified to act and let them address the need. It is unwise to attempt to revive someone using CPR if you do not know how to perform CPR. In purely practical terms, good-hearted people who see themselves as "Good Samaritans" can do more harm than good, if the responses they initiate are not suitable or well-coordinated.

With a handheld device and an Internet connection, it is easy to research any social challenge and access incredible quantities of information. Everyone can be a neighbour to almost anybody in the world. The 21st-century "Good Samaritan" is not the person who throws money around as a guilt reflex. It also is not the person who starts a "Go Fund Me" campaign for every cause that comes to their attention. One cannot be a Good Samaritan by participating in completely random acts of charitable largesse or by starting up a non-profit organization every time a social challenge appears.

In the context of the 21st century, a recommended "Good Samaritan" response when someone sees a problem is to find other people who are already at working to address that problem, rather than trying to initiate action without developing a sufficient understanding of the problem. We need to avoid duplicating efforts. Furthermore, it isn't always wise to act independently, particularly if organizations are already helping. If someone is drowning in a fast-flowing river and a lifeguard is already helping, it is not a good idea to jump into the water and attempt to "help" the lifeguard, particularly if you are a mediocre swimmer, or if you've never rescued anyone from a river. The kind of help that ought to be contemplated in this situation is supportive assistance. It would certainly be appropriate to call out to the lifeguard and ask how you can help. A qualified lifeguard might ask you to call 911 or execute some other task. It might be less dramatic, but it is likely to be far more effective.

> The reflex to help those who are in need has to be accompanied by the wisdom to know how best to ensure that appropriate help can be given.

The reflex to help those who are in need has to be accompanied by the wisdom to know how best to ensure that appropriate help can be given. If someone sees discrimination, poverty, or disconnection in the community, the best thing to do might be to contact an organization that is already at working on the issue and bring the observed problem to their attention. If there is exploitation or loneliness or injustice, it may be a good move to help existing organizations that are responding to these issues by contributing to them financially, volunteering with them, promoting their cause within our network of contacts, or joining the organization as a full-time team member. That is the essence of 21st century "Good Samaritanism."

1. Scripture quotations are taken from the *Holy Bible*, New Living Translation, copyright ©1996, 2004, 2015 by Tyndale House Foundation. Used by permission of Tyndale House Publishers, a Division of Tyndale House Ministries, Carol Stream, Illinois 60188. All rights reserved.

CHAPTER 4
What myths need to be exposed?

Aristotle maintained that women have fewer teeth than men; although he was twice married, it never occurred to him to verify this statement by examining his wives' mouths.
—Bertrand Russell

THE PROBLEM: We can unwittingly subscribe to fallacies and myths about the specific social challenges that community-based non-profit organizations seek to solve.

A Story About a Myth

In my days as a consultant, whenever I sat down to interview a prospective client, I had to confront a variety of myths. The main myth was a variation of the well-known joke that defines a consultant as the person who asks for your watch and then tells you the time. From time to time, a prospective client would offer the view that engaging a consultant is a completely unnecessary extravagance. A few senior executives even recited litanies of previous real or imagined failures of consultants and questioned the value of paying a consultant to tell them what they already knew. There were several instances where organizations that faced real headwinds in their markets confidently stated that all was well, and there was no need for outside help. They frequently believed these myths and defended them. Over the years, I developed a theory that those who needed my expertise the most were the least likely to engage my services.

This story is about an instance when an executive embraced a myth, but had the presence of mind to allow an outsider to determine if the myth he believed was, in fact, a myth.

Before proposing a scope of work in 2001, I had the opportunity to meet with the President of the company, a mid-sized American manufacturer. His primary concern was about achieving a sales breakthrough. The company sold its products via a variety of distribution channels and had only been able to attract second and third-tier players, rather than the best distributors in that industry. As part of the process of understanding the problem, I asked the executive what he believed was most important to distributors. Did he know what mattered to them? He listed ten to twelve things, and then I asked him to rank them by order of importance. He ranked price first, and the breadth of the product line second. His response was a bit surprising because I was aware that his organization did not routinely compete on price and that they did not offer a broad or innovative product line. Then I asked if he would be comfortable if I initiated a conversation with a cross-section of distributors to see if their answers were similar to his answers. He was wise enough to understand exactly what I was trying to do and decided that it wasn't a bad idea. At the same time, he expressed full confidence in his understanding of the principal concerns of his customers and prospective customers.

A month later, I returned with the results that had been collected. We put together a PowerPoint slide deck titled "What They Said." It came as a bit of a shock that virtually every belief he held about the perspectives of their current and prospective distributors was exposed as a myth. Without prolonging the story, the most important element, the one that drove the decision-making process of distributors, was the strength of the relationship with the manufacturer. The second most important thing was downstream sales support. The company had done next to nothing to this point to address either of these issues. They had embraced a price/product myth and wondered why their sales had stalled. Thankfully, they made the decision to embark on a process to address the needs and expectations of their distribution partners and, within a few years, they added new distribution channels and grew their business exponentially.

In the course of our progression to adulthood, we develop ways to frame information to allow us to understand the world. Sometimes these understandings are absolutely true and sometimes they are myths. A myth or fallacy is defined as a belief or understanding that is deceptive, misleading, or false, and often rooted in an unsound argument. There are many myths that frequently pass as accepted truth. Most of us have had the experience of believing something for a long time and then being forced to confront the reality that what we always understood to be true was not true. It can be the loss of innocence that comes with the realization that Mom is the tooth fairy, or that our parents put the presents under the Christmas tree. It can sometimes involve discoveries that are far more shattering and life altering. We can also find ourselves forced to confront beliefs about the realities that surround us, when we are invited to dispense with our preconceived biases and look at them carefully. Sometimes irrefutable facts are difficult to ignore.

> Most of us have had the experience of believing something for a long time and then being forced to confront the reality that what we always understood to be true was not true.

Our understanding related to the wide variety of social challenges we face in the 21st century is not exempt from myths. It is also not exempt from the phenomenon of oft-repeated myths that become accepted truths over time. Given the extraordinary amount of information that we are exposed to today, there is no end to the number of heart-breaking scenarios that even the most casual observer will be forced to confront. It is perfectly appropriate to look at a shocking miscarriage of justice, appalling social condition, or blatant discrimination, and be upset or angry about it. When any of us hear about (or observe) travesties like abuse, sex trafficking, the appalling treatment of First Nations populations, discrimination against those who identify in the LGBTQ2S community, child abandonment, homelessness, or hunger, we ought to recoil in horror. The problem begins when we believe a myth and then respond to a problem without grasping the reality of the situation or without seeking to understand its complexity. The result is that outrage is channelled into inappropriate responses. Anger and sadness are valid emotions, but if they are not combined with pragmatism and a plan that can be implemented, they can become the equivalent of "spitting into the wind."

> Anger and sadness are valid emotions, but if they are not combined with pragmatism and a plan that can be implemented, they can become the equivalent of "spitting into the wind."

Despite the overabundance of available information, there are still a number of myths and inaccurate perceptions that frame the way the public discourse unfolds around a variety of social challenges. We must ensure that we take appropriate steps to frame the tragedy or the preposterous situation in the context of the underlying root causes of the issue so that we are not buying into a myth and responding without first understanding.

The section that follows features four **social myths**. The review of each one is not comprehensive, and there are many more myths that need to be exposed. Why expose them? Simply put, if some of these myths continue to frame the thinking of those who are concerned about the disadvantaged, it is unlikely that an impetus for change will develop. Myths that stand in the pathway of potential solutions need to be shattered.

Social Myth #1 – The poor and disadvantaged are largely responsible for their situation.

Reality: Poverty in developed countries is the result of a combination of low wages, employment insecurity, inadequate education, chronic or untreated health problems, a racialized criminal justice system, and subtle discrimination.

For more than one hundred years, Western society has typically addressed the challenges of poverty and disenfranchisement with handouts and temporary remedies. The reaction is understandable, but these actions have not solved the problem. Some individuals can rise out of poverty, but poverty itself is not disappearing. The overall standard of living may have risen, but it has not risen equally. Researchers, activists, and politicians have proposed various macro-level remedies. None have been universally acclaimed. Ideas have included everything from the unrealistic to the utopian. Most countries in the world operate with an economy rooted in some form of modified capitalism. Most have constructed some sort of social safety net. In times of economic expansion, a social safety net may be left unquestioned, but when a country faces an economic downturn, there are immediate questions about why tax money is being used to support those who "should be required to support themselves."

For many years, there was a belief in a "natural order." Most people bought into the notion that an individual's economic situation was as it should be. It was accepted that some were destined to be poor and others were blessed with wealth. Immigration, particularly mass immigration to the United States, shifted the paradigm. Some people who had no opportunity for advancement in the Old World were able to discover opportunities in their new land, but wealth disparity continued, and successive waves of newcomers have had to endure discrimination and prejudicial realities.

Americans and Canadians continue to describe their countries as the kind of place where someone can become whatever they want to be. This isn't a lie, but it is a statement that needs to be carefully qualified; there are some limitations to the claim. A person who grows up in "the projects," and does not have access to good education or healthy food is far less likely to be in a position to become whatever they want to become. They are more likely to get involved with illegal activities or wind up in jail. They are far more likely to be unable to obtain work that will provide decent wages. Poverty is often a multi-generational phenomenon. There is a theoretical potential for people to gain traction socially and economically, but for many it remains highly theoretical.

The myth that has emerged is a variation of the "natural order" myth that existed more than one hundred years ago. In essence, it suggests that the poor are the authors of their own fate. This is often combined with resentment-laden statements that suggest that a huge portion of "my tax money" is turned over to chronically poor people in the form of welfare. The reality is that welfare payments represent 1-3% of government spending (depending on how it is measured). Anecdotes are recited about individuals who are able to discover ways to extract money from the system while avoiding any kind of hard work. Even if the stories are accurate, they are not representative. Research has consistently found that many people who live below the poverty line hold down more than one job to try to make ends meet. It also shows that most people do not enjoy receiving handouts.

> Statistics tell us that more than 45 million people in North America live below the poverty line.

Statistics tell us that more than 45 million people in North America live below the poverty line. 1 Many of these people are employed at low-wage jobs and yet they may have great difficulty making ends meet. This has caused us to coin the term "working poor." Some analysts may question the methodology that is used to determine the number of people who live below the poverty line or suggest that the statistical assessment of poverty is highly subjective. The point is that a large number of people live precariously. This is both a human tragedy and a major misappropriation of human talent. It is very difficult to extract oneself from poverty unless there is a system in place that facilitates the process. Is it possible to design a robust system to help prevent the seeds of poverty from taking root? Could energy be invested in seeking to eliminate the causes of poverty, rather than seeking to stigmatize the most vulnerable?

There are a number of bold ideas that have been tested in some jurisdictions. One of the more controversial ideas is the concept of a "guaranteed basic income." It aims to reduce the complexity of fuelling a variety of social assistance programs and, instead, ensure that citizens who qualify receive enough money directly from the government to maintain a healthy lifestyle. This is not a new idea. It dates back to the first Muslim caliph, Abu Bakr. Tests have been run in a variety of countries, most recently in places like France with the "RSA," China with a system that is called "dibao," and in Brazil, where more than 50 million families participate in the "Bolsa Familia" program. These plans appear to be oriented more towards welfare reform than poverty elimination, but they remain active elements of the social construct of each country.

There is something dreadfully wrong with a society where gun ownership is viewed as a constitutionally guaranteed right, but quality health care is reserved for the privileged or those who can afford insurance. Inadequate basic healthcare is often a contributor to poverty. At the very least, it is a companion of poverty. The poor lack agency, and they do not obtain the same level of care as the rich. Yet there is a substantial body of opinion that invites the poor to work harder and make better choices. They willingly ignore historical and environmental realities. Those who are poor cannot solve their own problems when the deck is stacked against them. The debate about where to put the blame has impeded the kind of discussion that could generate workable solutions. The easy course of action is to blame the victim and, in the next breath, give thanks for one's own good fortune.

Social Myth #2 – Emergency shelters are an entirely reasonable response to the challenge of homelessness.

Reality: Emergency shelters are just a patch and can contribute to the creation of a lifestyle of homelessness.

The typical approach of most large North American cities to the persistent social phenomenon of homelessness has been to create services for those experiencing homelessness, rather than dedicating efforts and resources towards eradicating homelessness. For well over 50 years, a "charity approach" has been the standard response to the broader challenge of chronic homelessness. The charitable reaction has involved setting up soup kitchens, financing dormitory-style emergency overnight shelters, and opening up church basements to serve the daytime needs of those experiencing homelessness. Well-meaning people even design "novel solutions"—like a backpack that folds out into a tent. People who find themselves homeless do not need fancy camping equipment. They need a permanent home. Interestingly, the general public tends to applaud "non-solutions" when they appear to be creative. The public may also be largely unaware that homelessness adds enormous costs to the healthcare system because people who spend an extended amount of time on the street inevitably end up putting increasing pressure on the capacity of the emergency rooms of hospitals. Importantly, those who spend a significant amount of time on the streets inevitably develop major health-related challenges that become costlier to treat with age.

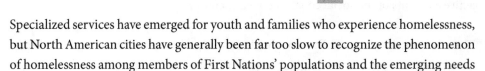

> People who find themselves homeless do not need fancy camping equipment. They need a permanent home.

Specialized services have emerged for youth and families who experience homelessness, but North American cities have generally been far too slow to recognize the phenomenon of homelessness among members of First Nations' populations and the emerging needs of the LGBTQ2S community—both of whom experience homelessness and exclusion at rates that are disproportionate to their population size.

Women's shelters generally have a slightly different vocation. They address the need for a safe place of respite for women who experience violence and abuse. Most offer a continuum of care as opposed to a brief "pit stop." These shelters are usually essential for purposes of protection and stabilization. They are often an effective first step on a path forward for those who make use of them.

Members of the public have also jumped into action in many communities. They organize drives to collect socks or blankets to give to those they encounter on the street. Some people decide to act alone and go out to parks to distribute food or clothing. As a charitable reflex, this feels good for the donor but does not appreciably alter the reality of the person being served. In most cases the help that is provided is disconnected from the real needs of the individual being helped. Ultimately, temporary comfort should not be divorced from steps that lead to permanent solutions. Life-saving measures are important but longer term actions need to be undertaken to prevent homelessness and to ensure that any experience of homelessness is brief.

> Temporary comfort should not be divorced from steps that lead to permanent solutions.

Homelessness can happen to anyone if there is a confluence of challenging life events. It can be caused by a series of events, circumstances, and choices. It doesn't usually happen suddenly; it is often a process, with a number of contributing factors. Some of these factors can be addressed preventatively. The primary driver of homelessness is isolation that drives profound social disconnection. This is often fuelled by mental illnesses, criminal activity, addiction, or behavioural abnormalities.

Most expert analysis has concluded that the challenge of homelessness has become more complex. Historically, when a town or city wanted to address homelessness, the reflex was to fund a network of emergency shelters. After all, people who are on the street or sleeping in parks need shelter, and there is an instinctive reaction to find a way to move the problem off the street and out of sight. It seems counterintuitive to suggest that this is a less than adequate response to the problem. Even more worrisome, emergency shelters can turn into a permanent way to manage those experiencing homelessness. A basic barebones shelter can be relatively inexpensive to run, particularly if it is funded largely through the generosity of donors. The problem is that it generates additional costs to taxpayers that are often overlooked. For example, the shelter system elevates the cost of policing and weighs down the judicial system. The outcome has been that the well-meaning actions typically undertaken in North American cities serve to hide or control individuals who are experiencing homelessness, but they are doing very little to resolve the problem of homelessness.

Over the past 50 years, emergency shelters have been insufficiently equipped to deal with the root causes of homelessness. Shelters can turn into an undignified patch on a problem that cries out for a permanent solution. At a typical emergency shelter, guests leave at 8:00 a.m. and return at check-in time, usually sometime between 2:00 and 5:00 p.m. Interestingly, the period between 8:00 a.m. and 5:00 p.m. is the best time for an intervention worker to meet with a client. Instead, at many emergency shelters, the client is sent back out into the street while the shelter cleans up and prepares for the next evening's realities.

Emergency shelters may have also contributed to the growth of panhandling in the downtown core of major cities. Why does panhandling exist? There are many reasons, and many of these are unrelated to the social challenges of homelessness because a proportion of the panhandlers are desperately poor, but not homeless. However, it is undeniable that the rhythm of life of an emergency shelter system dictates that someone who exits a shelter at 8:00 a.m. will need to spend their day somewhere, doing something.

The visible poverty of panhandlers, which has increased by many multiples in North American cities, has produced an additional social service called the "outreach worker." These people are often employees of a community organization that can secure some government funding. Street outreach work can also become the self-appointed private passion of well-meaning "lone wolf" volunteers who lack professional training. Virtually every outreach worker has good intentions. They can sometimes find vulnerable people who are hidden in culverts or living in dangerous locations. An outreach worker will try to ensure that a person who is experiencing homelessness gets water, food, and blankets. They may also refer or accompany someone to a location where they can obtain some basic health services. Street outreach instinctively focuses on harm reduction, a completely valid pursuit. The problem of typical outreach work is that there can be a disincentive to work one's self out of a job. Rather than facilitating connections to professional resources, there can be a temptation to concentrate on developing surface level relational connections with individuals, many of whom are not inclined to accept much help. Frequently, this is a function of workload. An outreach program that measures effectiveness based on the number of water bottles dispensed will end up focusing on activities rather than outcomes. When outreach work exists as part of a well-coordinated continuum of service, the life-saving service provided by an outreach worker can be very effective. When it is a disconnected or independent effort, it merely provides a bit of very temporary comfort to people in a state of homelessness or extreme poverty; a state that every rational person agrees is totally unacceptable.

Some people will wonder if generalized poverty reduction measures will automatically lead to a reduction in homelessness. Well-directed efforts to reduce poverty should be applauded because these initiatives have a ripple effect in reducing the prevalence of quite a few social challenges. The problem is that poverty reduction is not a universal cure. There is little doubt that acute poverty can contribute to the loss of stable housing, but the overwhelming majority of people who experience extended periods of poverty do not become homeless. The housing they obtain may be substandard, but it is a place to stay. Those who experience homelessness are usually poor, but poverty is rarely the primary cause of their predicament.

With all of the activity undertaken to try to help people who find themselves on the street, what results have been achieved? The answer is disappointing. Today, more people than ever are being charitable, but homelessness has grown in every measurable category. It continues to grow in most areas of North America. The approach to the problem needs to change. Rather than creating charitable services that cater to those experiencing homelessness, governments and CBNPs must develop a variety of pathways that lead to permanent housing. The key word is "variety." There is no single solution—no magic bullet. It may not be possible to prevent someone in North America from becoming homeless, but it is possible to stop doing things that contribute to him or her remaining in a state of homelessness.

Social Myth #3 – Food handouts are an appropriate response to food insecurity.

Reality: The underlying causes of hunger cannot be resolved using 20th-century tactics. The overall challenge of food security needs to be re-thought.

A growing challenge is the lack of understanding about how to respond to the problem of hunger and food insecurity, an unfortunate reality in most North American cities. A recently released comprehensive study [2] concluded that adults who experience food insecurity have a shorter lifespan. It is not a little bit shorter. The study suggests it is nine years shorter. Equally concerning is that those who are unable to obtain regular access to healthy food suffer from far greater incidences of chronic disorders, mental disorders, and suicide attempts. Food insecurity, clearly, is a contributing factor to unnecessary costs for the health care system.

So why do government agencies, donors, and community organizations that claim to be dedicated to eliminating food insecurity keep doing many of the same things when the results to date have been unsuccessful? Is it because nobody really "owns" the problem? Could it be that there is very little appetite for change? Alternatively, is it because the systems that are in place to respond to the problem are hopelessly ad hoc? Could it also be a consequence of the reality that a lot of good people with good intentions are fixated on delivering local charitable services that generate a lot of activity but are failing to eliminate the problem?

Some people believe that the problem of hunger is linked to the problem of food wastage. Waste is built into the pattern of food distribution and management. Some waste is inevitable, but modern Western nations have taken it to the extreme. Enormous quantities of perfectly good food are thrown away every day. In theory, this wasted food could be recuperated and distributed to those in need, but it cannot be done without a comprehensive supply management system, something that is challenging to implement without an effective local distribution system. Food waste begins at the producer level and continues with distributors, large institutions, hotels, restaurants, and grocery stores. Consumers are typically a little less guilty, but they continue the pattern. A recent assessment concluded that among 47 developed countries surveyed worldwide, the United States and Canada ranked first and third respectively for the amount of food wasted per capita. It is not a leadership position that should be a source of pride. The phenomenon of food waste is something that will require attention, but it is not the specific subject of this particular myth.

Interestingly, almost every North American city has more than enough surplus food to feed everyone; yet significant numbers of people are hungry. Verifiable numbers are not easy to obtain, but there is a fairly broad consensus that between 10 and 20% of the residents of major metropolitan areas in North America experience hunger or deprivation of healthy food on a weekly basis. The majority of these people have a place to live, but they exist at income levels below the poverty line. A Statistics Canada report on food security, updated in 2018, authored by Shirin Roshanafshar and Emma Hawkins concluded:

> *Every year from 2007 to 2012, there were more adults than children who experienced food insecurity. In 2011–2012, 10.2% of households with children and 7.6% of households without children were food insecure."* to "*Every year from 2007 to 2012, there were more adults than children who experienced food insecurity. In 2011–2012, 10.3% of households with children and 7.5% of households without children were food insecure.*

The hunger problem continues to grow despite the proliferation of the "classic" response—food handouts. Most cities have dozens, sometimes hundreds, of these operations. But this approach does not resolve the problem of hunger; it merely puts a temporary patch on it. It can be a temporary, somewhat undignified solution for people in need, but the evidence demonstrates that the number of hungry people isn't being reduced by their existence. When the activity of food handouts isn't reducing food insecurity in a community, we must ask ourselves if this is the best way to resolve the problem. Why do we have a reflex to create and sustain activities that respond to a symptom rather than a cause? What might occur if policy makers designed a framework that could dramatically reduce the need for people to be in a position where they had to resort to food banks?

> When the activity of food handouts isn't reducing food insecurity in a community, we must ask ourselves if this is the best way to resolve the problem.

The unparalleled growth of urban food handout systems, or food banks, has resulted in a phenomenon called the "food drive." A typical food drive promotes public awareness, but it is also one of the most inefficient forms of charitable giving. Why is it inefficient? Simply put, driving to a grocery store, purchasing a bunch of non-perishable items and putting into a bin that eventually needs to be collected, sorted and distributed is an exercise in misguided charity. To begin with, the major benefit goes to the grocery store. A grocery retailer is more than happy to profit from the sale of non-perishables. Good-hearted people seldom take into account that they are paying for these grocery purchases in after tax dollars. From an environmental perspective, a food drive generates a considerable carbon footprint, as small quantities of food move from place to place by car and truck. Then the sorting process engages large numbers of staff or volunteers, something that adds cost to the operation. Given that many of the donated products are not items that a hungry family really wants, there is additional waste.

The other part of the problem is that the experience of being handed a box full of miscellaneous non-perishables can feel humiliating. Asking for free food is an assault on a person's dignity, and being compelled to accept a handout just doesn't feel very good. People who need food want real food. They do not get excited about being handed a box full of cans of creamed corn, pasta, stewed tomatoes, or packages of things that they do not recognize. When people are given "food baskets" of miscellaneous non-perishables, they frequently discard many items they receive. They do not despise the charitable act, but they do not want to receive items that they know they will not use.

> People who need food want real food. They do not get excited about being handed a box full of cans of creamed corn, pasta, stewed tomatoes, or packages of things that they do not recognize.

The "food drive," as a way to respond to the problem of hunger, is something that will likely continue unless members of the public begin to understand that there is a far better way to achieve what they are aiming to accomplish. Donors might feel good about being involved in the process of giving something tangible, but they ought to be overjoyed to discover that there is a better way to achieve results that can produce a far greater impact. A direct cash donation to an efficient food security non-profit organization is far more beneficial than a few cans of non-perishables or random packages of pasta. Operationally effective food security operations can turn a $20 cash donation (for which a donor can usually obtain a tax receipt) into more than $200 of food that can be provided to those in need. Taking the tax-deduction into account, the donation costs the donor between $12 and $16 and provides more than $200 of assistance, while saving an enormous amount of time and energy. Also, a donor will reduce the environmental footprint that results from multiple pick-ups and drop-offs of small amounts of food.

People will frequently ask, "If we do not constantly conduct food drives, where will the food come from?" The answer is surprising to many, and it is linked to the myth that has persisted. The problem of hunger in North American cities isn't due to a shortage of surplus food. Food that is typically wasted in the value chain can be recuperated and redistributed if an efficient food management system is put in place. CBNPs that are trying to respond are locked into a charitable "food bank mindset" and are caught dealing with daily emergencies. There have only been sporadic attempts to take a step back and gain perspective. There have been even fewer attempts to harmonize activities between food security service providers.

Poverty and disconnection drive food insecurity, but traditional food banks and food counters are an inadequate response. They are a temporary fix that begs for a permanent solution that will respond to the real issue. The real issue is not hunger. Hunger is a symptom. Institutionalizing food banks, food counters or community kitchens is not the answer. It is a patch. Permanent solutions will include a change in the framing of government policy in order to reduce the number of people who are experiencing food insecurity. It makes no sense to create a massive response system to address a problem that could be fixed further upstream. A significant and comprehensive policy shift will also accelerate the transition process of people in need from dependence to independence.

Ideas similar to the introduction of a guaranteed basic income (briefly reviewed in Social Myth #1) are among the policy initiatives that need to be explored and piloted.

> It makes no sense to create a massive response system to address a problem that could be fixed further upstream.

Nonetheless, we cannot assume that it will be possible to completely eliminate food insecurity in North American cities, however, hunger can be greatly reduced if government agencies partner with innovative CBNPs and put a framework in place that incentivizes the recuperation of food and its rapid and effective redistribution. This also needs to be accompanied by a system that helps identify those who need assistance and provides them with a dignified way to receive the help they require. People who need to obtain food should be able to enjoy a shopping experience that is similar to a regular grocery store. They should not be forced to beg. They should also not be asked to line up at a food bank and accept a handout.

Social Myth #4 – Violence, prejudice, and discrimination exist, but they are typically blown out of proportion by the media.

Reality: Society is far more aware of prejudice and discrimination, but these problems do not appear to be in decline.

For the past 50 years, Western society has tolerated various forms of discrimination and violence by dismissing it as random and limited to a few deranged individuals who perpetrate reprehensible acts. This prevailing myth has permitted a sub-culture of acceptance of behaviours that should never be tolerated. It has been more or less socially acceptable, until recently, to utilize disrespectful language when referring to minorities or people who are on the margins. The use of racial epithets and slurs was more than mere jesting. It illuminated attitudes that translated into actions. Visible minorities and immigrants were treated in ways that we now consider to be largely unacceptable. Still, when modern-day leaders in Western countries refuse to call out racism, bigotry, and discrimination, it provides a licence to those who harbour discredited perspectives to propagate their beliefs.

There may not be more violence and discrimination in the 21st century when compared to previous centuries, but most people are more conscious of it because of the proliferation of stories in the media. CBNPs have emerged to address issues of senior care, abuse of children, sex trafficking, discrimination against visible minorities and immigrants, and the poor treatment of indigenous people. It is generally acknowledged that the roots of problems like poverty, inadequate housing, high-school dropout rates, and addiction are linked to an experience of exclusion or violence.

For many years, CBNPs were fighting an uphill battle due to significant gaps in the public's understanding of the troubling phenomenon of violence against women. In the 18th and 19th centuries, it was generally accepted that the kind of violence that was typically endured by women was a result of "male anger." Some scholarly articles in the 20th century even suggested that it was a function of a temporary loss of control. The idea was that, at a certain point, a man might reach his breaking point and snap. This gave rise to the notion that most men likely had a semi-logical reason that generated justification for them to lash out at their partners. The excuse for this display of anger was thought to be external factors like loss of personal social status or tensions in employment. Alternatively, male anger was dismissed as merely part of the relational tensions that were generated by disagreements about money or parenting, the discovery of infidelity, or the refusal of intimacy. Furthermore, a majority of the public was conditioned to look for blame on both sides when faced with a story about an abusive or violent incident. Violence in the home was considered a "private matter." There was, and still is, a tendency to ask why a smart woman would remain in an abusive relationship, hinting that the mere presence of the woman made her partly responsible for the outcome. As a result, solutions that were often advocated included therapy like couples counselling or similar tactics that were primarily designed to placate the abuser.

In the 21st century, many of the misunderstandings related to violence against women are being cleared up. To begin with, we have started to call it what it is. It is not a little "domestic problem"; it is violence. Research has concluded that this specific type of violence is rooted in a quest for absolute control. The perpetrator typically uses multiple techniques to inflict deep psychological trauma. Violence or abusive behaviour often begins in ways that can appear innocent, but it builds to a point where the victim is disoriented and confused. Meanwhile, the perpetrator often seeks to establish himself as the victim, in some cases claiming that he was merely fending off an attack or responding proportionately to a serious provocation. The outcome of violence is that the survivors of such abuse often have symptoms similar to post-traumatic stress disorder and require years of counselling on a long road towards recovery.

> The long-standing fundamental misunderstanding of the root causes of violence directed at women arguably hindered progress in addressing the problem.

The long-standing fundamental misunderstanding of the root causes of violence directed at women arguably hindered progress in addressing the problem. Those who work with women who are victims of violence will likely affirm the existence of other ongoing fundamental misunderstandings and that the change of attitudes is incomplete, even though the sentiments expressed in polite company in North America have shifted. It is a travesty that thousands of women in North American continue to be the victims of conjugal violence. This is a problem that must be resolved with a comprehensive approach. Building additional shelters and reforming the judicial system are necessary but they are an incomplete response to a problem that needs to be dealt with at its root. Some might argue that we are experiencing a renewed undercurrent of misogyny, prejudice, and violence that targets vulnerable minorities as we enter the third decade of the 21st century. Applying "patches" and dealing with emergencies as they occur is inadequate.

Aren't these myths just a function of differences of opinion?

The narrative that belies a myth can sometimes be subject to partisanship, meaning that there can be competing views about them. In many cases, they are, or ought to be, utterly non-partisan. There will always be perspectives that emerge in the mainstream, but are utterly unsubstantiated by facts. There will be claims and counterclaims, and some voices will be louder than others. The emerging of social media as a forum where opinions are exchanged has only served to further distort the issues that are at stake. The merits of different approaches to address specific social challenges can be debated, but the fundamentals should unite everyone. Why would anyone tolerate discrimination? Is it okay to stand by silently while someone threatens or ridicules a member of the LGBTQ2S community? Why are we not working harder to address the injustices that have created tensions within the communities of indigenous peoples and caused mind boggling inequalities to persist? Why does the judicial system fail to adequately protect vulnerable women and children from abusive or predatory men? Can we do better in addressing the challenges of isolated senior citizens? There are numerous examples of instances where opinions should align even if there is some debate on the methodology required to address the issue.

The phenomenon of veterans' homelessness is a perfect example of a complex social problem. It exists despite everyone's belief that it does not need to exist. There doesn't appear to be any credible opposition to the notion that every veteran should have a roof over their head. Yet, until recently, no single level of government—federal, state, or provincial—in the United States of America or Canada seized full responsibility for addressing it, nor is any single government department fully accountable for producing improved outcomes. There are dozens of factors that lead veterans to experience homelessness. Sometimes the trauma they experienced in combat zones causes them to disconnect from people. Some veterans struggle to maintain healthy relationships. This, in turn, can lead to a variety of addictions and/or precarious living. Veterans are often comfortable with social isolation, a common denominator in the processes that can result in homelessness. There isn't an easy, low-cost solution. However, there are a number of proven pathways that can lead a veteran from a life on the streets to a productive life in an apartment or other suitable dwelling, surrounded by a supportive community. The challenge is gaining a broad enough consensus so that concerted action can be taken.

The same is true for the problem of child poverty. Organizations that have sought to respond to this concern have typically employed a charity mindset and initiated a variety of programs like breakfasts at school, after-school academic help, and family crisis centres. Parents of these children are then encouraged to get free food at the local food bank, and sign their kids up for free sports programs at local community centres. Initiatives like these are fine charitable activities, but they have not measurably reduced child poverty. They simply put a patch on a growing reality.

So what is needed? The answer is a series of carefully coordinated actions that aim to eradicate the problem of child poverty. Many of the traditional tactics merely entertain the condition while encouraging charitable agencies to engage in actions that marginally reduce its impact. These actions cost money. They may be funded by generous donors or by government grants. We need to ask, is this the best way to address the problem?

When the majority of the actions taken in response to a complex social problem merely serve to manage the people who find themselves victimized by it, it is virtually certain that the problem will grow. Interestingly, the recently introduced Canada Child Benefit is an example of a concrete action that seeks to raise net family income for those living below the poverty line, and it appears, at least initially, to be having a measurable impact. According to recently updated data, the benefit served to lift more than 300,000 children out of poverty.

Why confront the myths?

These myths have created a series of misunderstandings that have affected the approach CBNPs have adopted. It is tough work for CBNPs to confront myths because it is often more convenient to benefit from them. If one confronts a myth it can become the beginning of a lonely battle. The impact of CBNPs has frequently been limited to patchwork because they struggle to keep up with the demand for patches, and they haven't been encouraged to develop an impetus to champion workable permanent solutions that take time and money to implement. They may add new services or make minor programming changes, but, in most cases, they have not successfully altered the status quo or substantially reversed the prevailing myths.

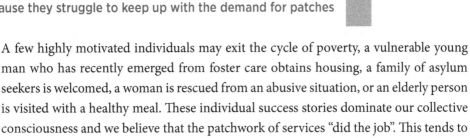

The impact of CBNPs has frequently been limited to patchwork because they struggle to keep up with the demand for patches

A few highly motivated individuals may exit the cycle of poverty, a vulnerable young man who has recently emerged from foster care obtains housing, a family of asylum seekers is welcomed, a woman is rescued from an abusive situation, or an elderly person is visited with a healthy meal. These individual success stories dominate our collective consciousness and we believe that the patchwork of services "did the job". This tends to anchor the myths in our consciousness. Meanwhile, local non-profit organizations hold fundraising events. Valiant efforts are made to gain media attention and lobby governments. Well-meaning people start new non-profit organizations that compete for space with existing non-profit agencies. Ultimately, the result of the prevailing myths is that there are more community-based non-profit organizations, more people doing good work—and an increasing number of people who are poor, hungry, homeless, violated, disenfranchised, or vulnerable.

Another narrative arises from a generally accepted belief that major social challenges ought to be resolved by equipping the victims to resolve the problem themselves. There are plenty of stories about individuals who "pulled themselves up by their bootstraps" and achieved success, despite overwhelming odds and seemingly insurmountable challenges. This is an accepted narrative that has formed the basis for countless fundraising campaigns, particularly as it relates to efforts to eradicate poverty via education or entrepreneurial endeavours. Some people stridently believe that any help that is provided to people must aim to help them help themselves so that they will not need outside help any longer. This philosophy, when applied in the extreme, can devalue efforts that legitimately provide short-term relief as a step towards a longer-term solution. There are instances when short-term fixes are needed before any longer-term plans can be put in place. Over the past decades, CBNPs have had some success with programs that aimed to increase literacy, address the delivery of basic health care, and develop jobs or entrepreneurial efforts. There isn't anything wrong with short-term relief when it is tied to a longer-term solution.

There are plenty of examples of solutions that eliminated the need for ongoing aid in situations where the former recipients of situational assistance became self-reliant and independent. Despite these cases, it is hard to argue that these programs alone have permanently altered the broad economic reality of a city or a region in a way that can be validated. Socially complex problems require solutions that go beyond simplistic responses like the often-repeated mantra of "teaching someone how to fish." In the context of North America, the way that government policies are framed either helps or undermines the efforts of CBNPs to address the challenges that exist.

The reality is that individual success stories that are rooted in myths serve to motivate a large number of donors. This keeps these myths alive. It is far easier to ask donors to respond to an urgent situation than it is to ask them to support a specific strategy that is part of a lengthy process designed to measurably reduce the impact of a complex social problem. What is worse is that the myths that have been outlined lead to fundamental misunderstandings about the role of community-based non-profit organizations.

1. https://www.povertyusa.org/facts

2. https://www.cmaj.ca/content/192/3/E53 - Association between household food insecurity and mortality in Canada: a population-based retrospective cohort study – Fei Men, Craig Gundersen, Marcelo L. Urquia, and Valerie Tarasuk

CHAPTER 5
Are there some prevailing misunderstandings about community-based non-profit organizations?

Most of the problems in life are because of two reasons: We act without thinking or we keep thinking without acting.
—Zig Ziglar

THE PROBLEM: Inaccuracies in the public discourse have caused community-based non-profits to develop misunderstandings about what they should do and how they ought to perform.

A Story About a Misunderstanding

I will not easily forget one of the most challenging assignments I undertook early in my consulting practice. It was one of those opportunities that a consultant eventually learns to avoid. Two well-known traps typically await the unsuspecting consultant who is contemplating any potential assignment. One is the trap of scope creep. This happens when a client asks the consulting firm to undertake a specific job, and then begins to add elements to it once the fee structure has been finalized and the work has begun. This is not unusual and, ordinarily, it is not a problem unless the consultant fails to identify the added work and gain the client's agreement to add that work and increase the overall cost of a project. The second trap is the client with misconceptions about the overall effectiveness of their organization. This happens when a potential client has perceptions about their requirements that range from sadly deficient to wildly delusional. What follows is a story about one of those clients (with all the names and the identifying details altered).

The disconnection should have been obvious to me at our first meeting, but it wasn't. Perhaps it was because I was a little too eager to help. Perhaps it was because this client had contacted us after hearing about successful similar initiatives we had undertaken with another company in that particular industry. In any event, the scope of work seemed clear, and the initial interview with the leader of the marketing group was cordial and informative. The problem became painfully obvious when we completed a more in-depth organizational needs assessment to ensure that the assumptions we were making were valid. This raised some red flags.

The proposed consulting assignment could best be described as the development of a process to train a group of employees. This cohort of employees was being established to respond to an emerging need within a business unit of a large organization. Given the nature of the industry, this particular assignment included some detailed design elements, considerable preparation for a training and orientation process, and some sequenced implementation to ensure success. All in all, it called for a fairly high level of organizational buy-in, but appeared to be entirely manageable.

Like any good consultant, I went to work preparing a document that summarized my understanding of the situation and suggested a series of steps to respond to the needs of the client. The problem was that I didn't know what I didn't know. Having received input from just one person, even though this was the group leader, I soon learned that this did not adequately inform me of the reality.

Unfortunately, the group leader who briefed me also had an incomplete understanding of the situation and of the ripple effect of the change that she was planning to implement. The group leader was functioning with a series of untested assumptions. She thought she was making a simple structural change in her group that, in the abstract, would permit her team to develop more meaningful relationships with key customers. This was compounded by an absence of any discernable understanding and buy-in for the initiative throughout the rest of the organization. There was strident opposition from a variety of supporting functions in the broader organization.

To begin with, the people directly involved had not been given any opportunity to understand the mechanics of the proposed change. They understood the reasons for the change, but everyone was able to articulate a number of internal roadblocks. This was generating unhelpful speculation on the part of the customer-facing team members that cascaded upwards to their managers. Ground level rumblings, in turn, created confusion and insecurity on the part of the team members who reported directly to the leader we were engaged with.

> The biggest problem was that the leader was utterly oblivious to the concerns and did not grasp the complexities of the changes she had decided to make.
>
> Ultimately, as much as this was a communication failure on the part of the leader, it was also an example of how the misconceptions or misperceptions of a leader can accelerate the trajectory of failure. Had the starting point included an understanding of internal realities and correct assumptions, the changes proposed would certainly have had a better chance of success. The plan would have unfolded differently. In the end, after a number of tense meetings and false starts, the change was abandoned and the assignment was discontinued. Shortly thereafter, the group leader was transferred laterally to a role in a different part of the organization.

"It ain't what you don't know that gets you into trouble. It's what you know for sure that just ain't so." This statement, often attributed to Mark Twain, is an appropriate starting point for this chapter. Why? Because it doesn't exist in any of Mark Twain's writings, nor is there any credible record that he said it. Nonetheless, it is often cited as part of the process of debunking misunderstandings. It is worth noting that the statement, on its own, rings true. People often believe things that are not true, and they sometimes cling rigidly to out-dated understandings or snippets of information that are only partly correct. Sometimes these incorrect beliefs are harmless. Sometimes they are mildly entertaining. But at other times, they are downright dangerous.

Classic 1970's half-hour TV situation comedies frequently developed their storylines through a series of compounded minor misunderstandings. The misunderstandings or misperceptions resulted in the protagonist or a sidekick creating an ever-worsening situation. The TV viewer was encouraged, by virtue of a "laugh-track," to chuckle at the series of communication pratfalls or relational tensions that flowed out of a very small slip up. The show would march along with a series of strangely comedic conversations and sight gags that were either hilarious or mildly amusing. Eventually, there would be a moment of clarity, and the episode would conclude with order being restored via an explanation or a discovery. This kind of script can produce laughs in a situation comedy, however, in the real world, misunderstandings don't typically produce barrels of laughs or resolve themselves neatly. Real life rarely mirrors a well-choreographed television program.

We all have mental models, ways that we frame information to allow us to understand the world. Like the leader in the consulting story described above, many people make decisions and initiate plans based on a series of misunderstandings or false assumptions. Non-profit organizations are not immune from this phenomenon. In fact, because they do not function with the pressure to provide monetary profits, they are more likely to be guilty of initiating action based on out-dated understandings or incomplete information.

Misunderstanding #1 – Every community-based non-profit organization should be "run on a shoestring."

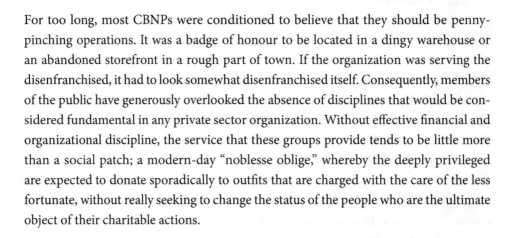

If the organization was serving the disenfranchised, it had to look somewhat disenfranchised itself.

For too long, most CBNPs were conditioned to believe that they should be penny-pinching operations. It was a badge of honour to be located in a dingy warehouse or an abandoned storefront in a rough part of town. If the organization was serving the disenfranchised, it had to look somewhat disenfranchised itself. Consequently, members of the public have generously overlooked the absence of disciplines that would be considered fundamental in any private sector organization. Without effective financial and organizational discipline, the service that these groups provide tends to be little more than a social patch; a modern-day "noblesse oblige," whereby the deeply privileged are expected to donate sporadically to outfits that are charged with the care of the less fortunate, without really seeking to change the status of the people who are the ultimate object of their charitable actions.

The problem with a social patch is that it peels away and needs constant repair or re-application. Even worse, many of the actors in the CBNP world have been conditioned to see themselves as a patch, or at least, act as if they are a patch. Au contraire! CBNPs should be expected to resolve issues. They should actively seek out new ideas to address an evolving landscape. They should be listening carefully to thought leaders so that they can implement innovative practices. They should also be expected to develop unparalleled operational excellence because it elevates the dignity of the people who are being served. CBNPs should be taking actions that are thoughtfully designed to produce a measurable reduction of social scourges like child abuse, hunger, violence against women, chronic homelessness, discrimination against the LGBTQ2 community, and isolation of senior citizens.

The accepted historical practice has been to dismiss any failures or inefficiencies in community-based non-profit organizations as inevitable or completely forgivable. Members of the public typically accept that non-profit work is a little bit messy. A great deal of the non-profit work is messy and unpredictable. When a community group is serving food to the hungry or welcoming the most disadvantaged into a day-centre, things are never straightforward or predictable. In any emergency shelter, youth crisis centre, or harm reduction facility there will be things that go sideways every day. However, that is not an excuse for sloppiness or ineptitude. It is not a reason to resist assessment or to avoid accountability. It is not an excuse to ignore the need for key financial controls or to fail to keep abreast of the best clinical practices. The nature of the human challenges that these organizations deal with can produce a somewhat chaotic working environment, but this isn't a reason for tolerating organizational chaos. When an organization declares that it exists to serve those in need, it needs to do so with excellence. Those in difficult circumstances deserve nothing less than the best.

> The accepted historical practice has been to dismiss any failures or inefficiencies in community-based non-profit organizations as inevitable or completely forgivable.

For the past 100 years, the public has largely ignored the shortcomings of the community-based non-profit sector because these groups existed to address problems that society or governments did not want to own. The sector was left alone. Their actions were rarely questioned because they were assumed to be the experts in handling challenging social issues. Good-natured people nodded approval to them and tossed a few coins their way at Christmas, Easter, or Thanksgiving. Sure, there have been occasional investigations into their practices and, every once in a while, an enterprising reporter will turn up evidence of serious misdeeds or financial irregularities in a non-profit organization. Some of the better-known scandals have included overpaid executives, poor treatment of clients, or toxic working environments. These problems are often the result of poor oversight, a lack of attention to a problematic culture, or a leader who has gone rogue. These isolated scandals came and went away. The bigger scandal might be why there is a pervasive expectation that a vastly underfunded network of CBNPs is expected to operate with underpaid people and limited resources.

Misunderstanding #2 – Anyone can start and run a community-based non-profit.

One of the obvious challenges for a CBNP is the need to attract insightful leadership so that sound management disciplines are in place (a topic that will be covered in a subsequent chapter). When the annual revenue of a CBNP exceeds two million dollars, there is usually a need to recruit well-qualified and experienced management talent. This means hiring people who may not have a background working on the front lines of a community organization. With no disrespect intended, most community organizers and professional social workers are not trained or experienced in the world of business, finance, or management. If an organization owns or rents buildings or other infrastructure, it may also need to recruit people who are qualified to manage these assets. When a CBNP hires salaried or hourly staff, there will be routine HR concerns and legal and government requirements that need to be managed by qualified people. If an organization runs programs or serves meals, it needs trained professionals to oversee logistics and manage a kitchen efficiently. It takes people and assets to deliver services. This fundamental principle is no different in the for-profit sector than it is in the non-profit sector.

When a community organization gets started, the founders rarely give much thought to the structure that will be needed or the management philosophy that they will employ. The immediate goal is simply to help people in need. After a few years, a CBNP will arrive at a point where things begin to veer out of control because an inevitable conflict occurs between the need to focus on the services provided on the front line and the need to manage people, revenues, and expenses so that services are not disrupted.

> Non-profit management is challenging—good intentions or a sense of outrage about a particular issue simply isn't enough.

There is a prevailing belief that any good-hearted person who can identify a noble cause can start up and run a non-profit. Nobody wants to believe that the people who try to help others might miss the mark. The truth is that non-profit management is challenging. Most people would expect that the hard part is linked to generating awareness and raising funds. Both are indeed challenging, but it is even more challenging to ensure that the actions of a CBNP—its efforts, services, and programs—generate outcomes that are aligned with the declared aims of the organization. It calls for management experience and leadership skills because good intentions or a sense of outrage about a particular issue simply isn't enough.

Misunderstanding #3 – Community-based non-profit organizations can't be held accountable for results.

CBNPs tend to avoid stressing too much about formulating plans based on sound assumptions that are grounded in measurements, verifiable data, and facts. The need for accurate facts in the sector has been overlooked for many years because the scope of the operations of many local efforts is so small that there is little impetus to dedicate resources to the discipline of data collection. Verifiable data often needs to include case files and a computerized system that can identify patterns and trends while ensuring anonymity in the analysis. If an organization typically serves 40 to 80 individual people each week in a specific local geography, they are unlikely to invest in any quantitative analysis because they rely on the memories and recollections of the staff and volunteers. They usually know everyone they serve by their first names and have little reason to develop recordkeeping, databases, or electronic clinical files. A local drop-in centre may count people who come in each day, but if there is any rotation of staff, individual guests can be counted three or four times in a day if they enter, depart, and return several hours later. This can unrealistically inflate the scope of some challenges.

The collective wisdom of key people in the CBNP and their general sense of how things are going becomes a barometer of on-the-ground realities. Collective wisdom is important, but it paints an incomplete portrait of the situation unless it is accompanied by reliable data. Collective wisdom and anecdotes can lead to the creation of urban myths. There have been numerous examples of "facts" that were widely believed and that were discovered to be less than factual when they were confronted by scientific research.

There is also a general misconception around the measurement of the performance of non-profit organizations. A for-profit organization needs to generate a measurable return on the assets invested by its shareholders. Some people believe that a non-profit is exempt from that requirement. In the most classic sense, a non-profit will not be measured by the monetary profit it generates or by its return on capital invested. However, it does need to produce a return on the investment of its funding agencies and ought to be held accountable for results. It isn't easy to quantify metrics for outcomes in the language of accounting. Nonetheless, in the 21st century, investors in CBNPs should be demanding that CBNPs clearly identify measurable outcomes and community impact. How else can we know if anything is changing?

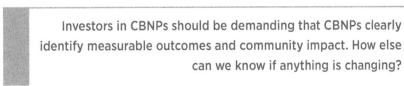

> Investors in CBNPs should be demanding that CBNPs clearly identify measurable outcomes and community impact. How else can we know if anything is changing?

If money is invested, what outcome can we reasonably anticipate, and is the outcome cost-effective? This may require the development of new metrics of performance and could include impact measurements that have not been used in the past.

If funding is provided to supply low-cost housing to those who need it, how can we evaluate whether the funds are delivering results?

If an investment is made to provide after school support to at-risk young people, can we measure the impact of the effort and compare it to the costs associated with the high-school dropout rate?

If a food security operation is funded in a particular neighbourhood, will it measurably deliver an increased level of health and wellness in the area?

If a drop-in centre is built to address the needs of specific at-risk population groups, how can we evaluate if it is an effective tactic to respond to the core needs of that community?

The common denominator for all of these questions is that they do not evaluate activities. They seek to assess impact. Activities count, and CBNPs need to collect statistics that quantify activities. It is important to know how many people came to a drop-in centre, how many families accessed a subsidized housing program, how many immigrants obtained hot meals at a local drop-in center, and how many seniors received in-home care last week. The problem is that this information, on its own, does not adequately inform us. Increases or decreases in any of these numbers do not measure impact or effectiveness.

Many people believe that any "good" thing that can be accomplished is a worthwhile thing. However, good is the enemy of great. Most CBNPs focus on doing "good work" and avoid assessments, measurements, verifiable data, and facts. The slogan might well be: "Who needs facts and measurements when there is a waiting list for our services, and when people line up to get into our facilities?" The default is to go straight to work. Without the pressure to produce monetary profits, CBNPs are more likely to be guilty of initiating action based on out-dated understandings or incomplete information.

> Who needs facts and measurements when there is a waiting list for our services, and when people line up to get into our facilities?

Accountability is important because many of the objectives for CBNPs are long-term and evolving. As an example, organization ABC may claim to be dedicated to eradicating poverty in a specific geography. What should be done if their actions do not actually produce any meaningful change in the poverty level of the area over a period of time? The typical reflex is to find environmental factors and place the blame there. Environmental factors include issues like lack of housing due to the process of gentrification, the local rate of unemployment, chronic poverty, or an increase in the number of immigrants.

In other cases, legitimate cause and effect can be tied to a specific government policy or the cancellation of a specific social initiative. It should also be legitimate to call the activities of organization ABC into question, and ask if they are doing the right things. There should be a willingness to review their strategy and tactics. It has to be acceptable to wonder if some of the things they are doing merely help maintain people in poverty. The problem is that if someone has the temerity to raise the issue of CBNP effectiveness, they are sometimes labelled as an intolerant malcontent. It ought to be perfectly legitimate to explore whether organization ABC is taking steps that could actually result in an elimination of the need for them to exist. If they are, then they should be anticipating an evolution of their services or the closure of their operations. Success should mean that they would no longer be needed in the area. Very few organizations ever sit down and write up an action plan that assumes that they will go out of business but, if a persistent social condition were resolved per the objectives of a CBNP, wouldn't it be reasonable to have a plan in place that assumes their organizational demise?

Misunderstanding #4 – Any kind of charitable activity is a good thing.

This misunderstanding is at the root of a number of less than ideal responses. Chapter Three makes the point that a charitable act without any follow-up does not resolve a situation. The idea is that any kind act of charity is always a good thing when, in fact, charity can be very destructive in certain circumstances. Charity on its own cannot resolve complex social problems. Complex social problems are multi-dimensional challenges that cross a variety of jurisdictions.

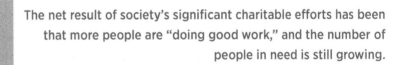
The net result of society's significant charitable efforts has been that more people are "doing good work," and the number of people in need is still growing.

For the past 50 years, well-meaning people have tried, without success, to use the principles of charity to address major social problems. Despite intense and sustained formal and informal charitable efforts, the social challenges are greater than ever in North America. More people experience violence, more people experience homelessness, more people are isolated, more people are hungry, and more people experience discrimination and an absence of agency. At the same time, more CBNPs have emerged and more people are employed in the charitable sector. To put it another way, the net result of society's significant charitable efforts has been that more people are "doing good work," and the number of people in need is still growing.

A typical response to this phenomenon is to blame societal factors and government policies. Both are certainly contributors. Governments have been woefully inept in framing policy in most jurisdictions. However, when the approach at the point of care is suboptimal, it is important to acknowledge it and not point to the failures of others. Those in the CBNP sector must own up to their own shortcomings and not constantly point the finger at any other guilty parties.

What can charity accomplish or achieve? The short answer is that charity can provide immediate relief or assistance, provided the problem is one dimensional and has a limited scope and time frame. Charity can be particularly effective as a response just after a disaster strikes. There are a few very specific situations where a spontaneous charitable action is the best possible response. In many cases, it is the worst possible response. Where is charity the best response? If an apartment building burns down overnight, a river is threatening to overflow and flood a city, or a tornado cuts a swath of destruction through a neighbourhood on a Saturday morning, charitable actions may be the best reaction. Charitable efforts kick into gear in the face of natural disasters all the time. Charity can also be very effective in the face of a pandemic. Goods are assembled, resources are marshalled, necessities are distributed, and shelter is provided, often without fully developing detailed operational plans. What matters most is the ability to act quickly and decisively with the basics like food, water, shelter and medicines. When the disaster persists, like the recent situations in Haiti and Puerto Rico, the public quickly experiences the limitations of any charitable reflex, particularly if it is combined with inept planning, systemic corruption, or social complexities. Charitable efforts can also be complicated by confusion that occurs during a rapidly evolving situation.

Few people would dispute the potential effectiveness of charitable actions as a response to a disaster or a major emergency. Charitable approaches can be helpful, in the short term, even when the actions undertaken are spontaneous or less than perfectly orchestrated. With the 24-hour news cycle, everyone can witness the frustrations of spectacular failures when ineptitude and poor execution combine to turn charitable efforts into debacles. Nevertheless, a spontaneous, charitable action can occasionally be the best response to imminent danger or a threat, when that action will save a life or remove someone from peril.

A number of metaphors have been popularized over the years to contrast the isolated charitable act of giving with the process of resolving a systemic problem. Everyone has been exposed to some version of the accepted wisdom that it is better to teach someone to fish than to hand out fish. The validity of this truism largely depends upon the scope and urgency of the problem. There are situations that require an emergency solution before any other solutions can be contemplated. If someone is starving, it is important to feed them before teaching them to develop methods that will allow them to generate their own supply of food. To follow along with the metaphor, there are plenty of situations where it is appropriate to supply fish as an interim measure before determining if there is a reasonable opportunity to catch some fish nearby.

The bottom line is that the basic charitable model is scandalously deficient in situations where the problem is systemic and complex. Despite this, most North American CBNPs that seek to address persistent social conditions stubbornly continue to follow a charitable model. They follow it even though the outcomes produced are suboptimal. Why are CBNPs making this error? It's probably because everyone is very comfortable with being charitable. Donors appreciate the efforts of those who are on the front lines addressing pervasive social issues. There is an increasing level of demand for the services that CBNPs provide. The people who are leading the effort are validated by the media and by politicians as important providers of services to the vulnerable. Additionally, traditional charitable efforts will almost always produce some mildly impressive preliminary results, or at least, results that can be made to appear impressive. What is the result of clinging to the charitable model? It is that significant amounts of donors' money and resources are being applied to the wrong activities, and some of the outcomes have not been ideal.

> Significant amounts of donors' money and resources are being applied to the wrong activities, and some of the outcomes have not been ideal.

Charity is usually rooted in empathy and kindness. Nobody should make a case against kindness. As humans, we ought to have a human reflex that flows out of kindness. To dismiss kindness is like speaking against motherhood, apple pie, and small puppies! The act of assisting other human beings without self-interest is, or ought to be, a core human quality. If anyone sees an injured person or a hungry child, the instinctive response ought to be one of empathy. That said, it is perfectly appropriate to question how to translate the most human of feelings into effective action. The question is not whether people should feel charitable. The question is how charitable feelings should motivate someone to take effective action when they are faced with a complex need or an emerging and tragic social phenomenon. What realities should inform our thinking? What are the most appropriate actions to take? What should people avoid doing so that they end up being helpful rather than harmful?

Over the years, particularly in North America, a mindset about charity and charitable giving has been cultivated. Some people see charitable actions as a duty because their parents taught them to be sensitive to the less fortunate and to give back. Some even apply specific principles and disciplines of giving that have been incorporated into broader methods for managing personal finances. For example, there are some who have developed a habit of setting aside a specific percentage of their income for the purposes of making charitable donations. Others take a "me-first" approach and give sporadically. Others have an inward focus that propels them to be deeply suspicious of almost any cause or perceived need. They have heard of scams, and they don't want to be deceived by a fraudster masquerading as a person in need! So they ignore the disabled person in the wheelchair selling pencils at the door of the grocery store, and they pretend they do not see the young woman who is sitting in a corner in the subway with a sign that says, "Any amount of money will be helpful." They may even believe that those in difficulty ought to "get their act together." Others wonder aloud if social programs or assistance efforts cater to people who routinely abuse the system.

Pointing everyone in the right direction

How can a government funding agency, a donor, or an investor avoid being caught in these prevailing misunderstandings? How can we be kind without buying into a model that repeatedly puts patches on the problems? What factors can help determine whether a community-based non-profit is likely to deliver a return on investment? These are questions that ought to be asked more frequently.

A number of major funders have initiated studies that have produced measurements or tests to evaluate the overall effectiveness of CBNPs. In some cases, funders have reduced or eliminated their support when CBNPs rank at the bottom of a particular cohort, or when they fail to meet specific metrics. This is not a bad idea if the metrics are reasonable and relevant. A careful examination of six important indicators may eliminate some misunderstandings and illuminate the things that anyone contemplating offering financial support to a CBNP should consider. There are plenty of other indicators, but these six are a good place to start.

Indicator 1: Does the community-based non-profit orient its services based on up-to-date evidence-based information? Many non-profits simply respond to those in need and have not established any disciplines around using research or indicators to fine-tune their operation. Access to relevant data can sometimes confirm the observations of those who are in the action day after day. Solid real-time data improves decision-making. Rather than having to make decisions based on anecdotes or historical practices, organizations that are serious about delivering quality services that respond to real and emerging needs will seek out best practices that are anchored in research, and evaluate how to implement them. The best CBNPs are passionate about understanding who they are serving and why the need exists, and seek out evidence that will inform them of shifting needs. They are also unafraid to put a stop to programs that are ineffective, and experiment with new ways of doing things.

> The best CBNPs are passionate about understanding who they are serving and why the need exists, and seek out evidence that will inform them of shifting needs.

Indicator 2: **Is the community-based non-profit focused on objectives and impact?**
Most non-profits talk at length about their actions and activities, like the number of people they have fed or the number of packages they have distributed. They may also describe the growth of problems that they are addressing. Websites, communication tools, and annual reports of these organizations often include a long list of their noble actions or activities. Some have called it the "WE song." "WE do this, and WE do that!" There is nothing wrong with tallying up activities however the ability to undertake day-to-day activities in response to a social concern does not automatically equip an organization to identify how to resolve a persistent social problem. Equally, an acceleration of activities does not mean that the organization is making progress. Most CBNPs love to trumpet things like the number of attendees in a specific program, the number of nights of shelter provided, or the amount of free clothing distributed. These activities are held up as proof of the organization's response to unacceptable social problems and the ongoing need for donor support. More activity is not a sign that objectives are being met or that their programs and actions are contributing to the resolution of an unacceptable situation. In the private sector, nobody would tolerate enterprises that tried to pass along activity-based measurements as proof of their viability. Imagine a retail store declaring that it was a roaring success based on a daily report that measured nothing except the total number of clients that came through their front door. A store that doesn't evaluate other more critical metrics—number of sales transactions, total sales by category, average revenue per customer, and profitability—would be guilty of basing investment and management decisions on the wrong data.

> More activity is not a sign that objectives are being met or that an unacceptable situation is improving.

Measuring activities in a CBNP ought to be undertaken to understand the scope of the day-to-day rhythm of the organization. However, activities alone do not produce tangible results or lasting impact. It is vital that CBNPs ensure that all activities are carefully targeted, grounded in facts and data, and evaluated with the objective of producing measurable outcomes. Donors need to dispense with the notion that any effort should be supported if it engages emotionally, and if the CBNP can point to a growing list of activities. Everyone needs to ask themselves if anything is changing as a result of what the organization is doing. This may require some CBNPs to develop new metrics that measure how their important activities are contributing towards the outcomes that they claim to be targeting. It may also result in discoveries. When any organization undertakes some self-examination, it will inevitably uncover some activities that should be changed or eliminated.

Indicator 3: Is the community-based non-profit unselfishly building partnerships to leverage their achievements? There is a "lone wolf" reflex in the DNA of many CBNPs. Several organizations may campaign independently for precisely the same cause and resolutely refuse to align their activities with each other. Progress typically happens when there is well-orchestrated ongoing collaboration among high-capacity organizations that can harness resources in a complementary fashion. This requires a significant shift in thinking and an unswerving commitment to a process that isn't easy. Partnerships are not always easy to form, and they are challenging to nurture. Yet they are essential to resolving complex social challenges and the fastest way to achieve major breakthroughs. A collection of misaligned organizations will never achieve what a few well-funded and well-aligned organizations can accomplish.

> Progress typically happens when there is well-orchestrated ongoing collaboration among high-capacity organizations that can harness resources in a complementary fashion.

Indicator 4: Is the community-based non-profit listening to voices that transcend the predictable chorus of stakeholders? Sure, all stakeholders matter, but many individual stakeholders will lack a wider perspective. If a non-profit listens only to its primary stakeholders, it may fall into the typical trap of always doing what one specific stakeholder thinks should be done. There are instances where a CBNP needs to go beyond what its clients or its donors say if they want to provide the kind of services that are needed. The strength of solid organizations is in being able to correctly interpret the realities of the present and respond to them with an eye to the future. Leading non-profit organizations gather information and ideas broadly, seek to identify trends and best practices in other jurisdictions, and uncover potentially innovative solutions that can be adapted to their local needs.

Indicator 5: Is the community-based non-profit disciplined about improving their value proposition in tangible ways year after year? Many organizations place a very high value on "the cause," but they do not invest in the management disciplines that are essential to serve it. Far too often, CBNPs make excuses for sloppy practices. Usually the reasons—or excuses—centre on a lack of money. There is a mindset of scarcity and a belief that they will never have a big enough budget. This mindset leads to an absence of excellence because the organization provides itself with an escape clause. Once it becomes okay to be a bit mediocre in one area, it is easier to become convinced that mediocrity is all that there is. This sort of defeatist thinking can become part of the culture, and it affects any attempts to be creative in programming and the delivery of services. Then the organization loses the impetus to improve or update the simple things that they need to address to continue to be relevant. CBNPs that are committed to making real change happen are constantly searching for areas where they can improve. Some improvements do not require money. Most improvements actually save money.

> Once it becomes okay to be a bit mediocre in one area, it is easier to become convinced that mediocrity is all that there is.

Indicator 6: **Is organizational survival a dominant part of the ongoing fundraising pitch of the community-based non-profit?** Most CBNPs passionately articulate a desire for change. They want to accomplish big things like ending discrimination, eliminating the exploitation of women and children, stopping sex trafficking, ensuring that nobody is hungry, making education and literacy accessible to everyone, or providing essential vocational training that results in permanent employment. The aims are lofty and well intentioned. The problem is that the narrative that donors hear is about the need to survive. Many organizations orient their communication in a way that highlights the urgent need for a cash infusion that will prevent them from being forced to close their doors. There is usually a primal instinct for a community-based non-profit organization to fixate on its survival, and this can cause it to fail to conduct the most cursory assessments of its ongoing relevance.

> There is usually a primal instinct for a community-based non-profit organization to fixate on its survival, and this can cause it to fail to conduct the most cursory assessments of its ongoing relevance.

One of the realities linked to the survival of any CBNP is the need to attract and retain donors. There is nothing wrong with the reflex to fundraise nor is it wrong to try to obtain donor-partners to fund programs and achieve important goals. The challenge is that there is very little motivation for a CBNP to inform their donors about the complexity of the issues they are seeking to address. The accepted wisdom is that this does not work. Donors love to read about dramatic stories that recount the progress of individuals rather than dry data or pages full of facts. This has led organizations to hire professional writers who construct and embellish anecdotes that are designed to attract certain types of donors. There is nothing wrong with telling success stories. They matter. Still, some organizations take this to the limit of good taste by sending fundraising letters that border on the sensational. They may highlight the story of a young person who couldn't afford to go to school, but thanks to "donors like you"| has now become a medical professional. This kind of exceptional story often forms the crux of the argument for continuing to fund programs. Cue the television commercial that starts with images that evoke sympathy and begs for "just a few dollars a day" to ensure that the non-profit organization can generate more of these success stories.

A prevailing strategy has been to appeal to donors by highlighting urgent organizational needs. A CBNP may routinely send out communiques that highlight impending cash shortages or the potential termination of a program if a certain amount of money is not raised by a particular date. This tactic becomes suspect if it is routine. One reasonably well-respected CBNP sends out a year-end letter every year describing its impending deficit position and appealing for an urgent response. Donors increasingly tire of hearing about an organization's needs. Donors should not donate because an organization has needs; they should give because the organization is able to **meet** unmet needs of the people they serve.

> Donors should not donate because an organization has needs; they should give because the organization is able to meet unmet needs of the people they serve.

Some CBNPs spend a lot of energy on activities meant to ensure survival. This philosophy often includes a resistance to change because the leaders have very little time to pause and reflect. They are often sceptical of new information that comes to light, particularly if it challenges their strongly held beliefs. This happens because they have anchored their efforts in a rigid framework and any kind of major shift in thinking represents an existential threat. On the other hand, CBNPs that are progressive have a laser-like focus on providing the best solutions based on evolving client needs. This kind of organization will typically partner with researchers and universities to conduct studies that employ scientific methods. They may run pilot programs and test out new ways of doing things. They are usually candid about their shortcomings, and they work towards improvement. These CBNPs tend to be nimble and solution-oriented and are less concerned about their longevity.

Every CBNP should challenge its underlying assumptions regularly. It is vital to determine if the needs they believe they are responding to are still relevant needs. This is where a culture of measuring the things that matter will make a major difference. Unmet community needs tend to evolve year after year, and organizations can sometimes find themselves running programs that do not provide the best possible services to their clients. Often the clients themselves simply get used to the service, and neither the client nor the service provider is capable of imagining anything different.

Sometimes it takes an external issue to put an end to ineffective efforts. If a building burns down, a lease is terminated, a key volunteer departs, or a critical piece of equipment breaks and the repair cost is astronomical, programs that were once thought to be indispensable are often abandoned, and everyone discovers that there is a completely different way to achieve a similar outcome. In several well-documented cases, a major calamity forced an organization to radically alter their service offering, and the result was an enormous improvement that would have never happened without the catalyst of the crisis.

How do the best CBNPs address misunderstandings? This is where leadership plays an important role. An organization with ineffective leadership will wallow in misunderstandings and fail to evolve as needs change. Enlightened leaders are able to envision how the organization can move past these misunderstandings and avoid being imprisoned by a false narrative. This is why leadership is critical.

CHAPTER 6
Why does leadership matter?

A real leader uses every issue, no matter how serious and sensitive, to ensure that at the end of the debate, we emerge stronger and more united than ever before.
—Nelson Mandela

Change happens at the speed of trust.
—Stephen M.R. Covey

THE PROBLEM: There is an emphasis on compassionate activism within community-based non-profit organizations and an absence of emphasis on the competencies and disciplines of leadership.

In my 14 years as a consultant, I had the opportunity to work with many organizations in different industries. Prior to any assignment, when initially interviewing executives and C-suite leaders of a particular company, I discovered that people who had worked in a particular business for most of their careers felt that there was a profound uniqueness about their particular business. Pharmaceutical executives would say that their challenges were vastly different compared to issues that I might have seen in banking, distribution, hospitality, or manufacturing.

Given that my work exposed me to many different industries, it became clear that every single business challenge, no matter the sector, centred around four general areas: capitalization, products or services, customers, and leadership. In privately held companies, there was the additional concern of ownership intention; for example, issues could emerge if the major shareholder was looking to monetize the asset in the near term. For every organization, the realities of rapidly evolving external environments factored into the four general areas of challenge. Changes in the landscape have a real impact on use of capital, product life cycles, customer loyalty, and the engagement of employees. The size of the organization, while important, was seldom a major factor. Most of the time, size simply added layers of complexity to the fundamental challenge, or it dictated the speed with which a shift in direction could be executed. I had the occasion to work with start-up companies that had sales of less than 10 million dollars, all the way up to large organizations with market capitalization in excess of 100 billion dollars.

Over the years, I developed a set of questions that I used to identify and triangulate on the challenges. Many of these questions are centred on leadership and the exercise of leadership at all levels in an organization. My observations have caused me to conclude that one of the biggest differentiators among organizations is excellence in leadership.

It is important to note that great leadership on its own will not guarantee success. A great CEO will not be able to guide an organization that is inadequately capitalized, is marketing products that nobody wants, or has a toxic culture any more than a great captain will be able to steer a ship that has a large hole in it. Having said that, when the fundamentals are sound, the big differentiator is the exercise of effective leadership.

I have had the privilege of working with some great leaders in the course of my career. I have also observed people who were in a leadership role, but had no ability to lead and simply exercised positional power.

A Story About Ineffective Leadership

> I will never forget Dean (not his real name). He was one of the most cerebral CEOs that I ever met. He was well educated and made very sure that anyone who met him knew about it. Everyone respected him for his subject-matter mastery of a variety of issues. On virtually any technical issue in his industry he would be the "go to" person in the room. He was admired among his peers for his ability to absorb and explain scientific and technical details that had commercial implications. His expertise provided him with a profile that was the envy of many. However, intelligence and wisdom are not synonymous.
>
> Dean's grasp of technical issues and his ability to systematically process complex issues were impressive, but these capabilities did not make him a great leader. The board of the company thought that someone who was as smart as Dean would naturally be an outstanding leader. The problem was that he never should have been leading an organization because his technical excellence did not prepare him for the human dimension of leadership. Dean was fine with pieces of paper and complicated diagrams. As soon as people entered the equation, he fell apart as a leader. In critical situations, he was unable and unwilling to confront people who were working at cross-purposes in his organization. To begin with, he lacked courage. A fairly evident flaw was that he was strangely paranoid about developments in his industry. Dean would frequently call me and demand my view on situations that

featured various amounts of conjecture and monumental leaps in logic. He would outline how if "A" happened, then "B" would almost certainly follow. This, in turn, would mean "C" and "D," and by the time he got to "E" or "F," his organization had been outmanoeuvred by a complexity in the supply chain, or his competition was pricing him out of a particular market. I cannot remember how many times I talked him out of making ill-conceived telephone calls to competitors or sending emails he would have regretted.

Dean was unable to lead in a coherent way because his lack of courage often resulted in tentative decisions that he reversed, and then reversed again. He frequently listened to people who reinforced his misinformed or mildly warped perspectives. For a number of years, his company experienced solid growth that was largely attributable to the growth curve of the industry. All the companies in that industry were taking advantage of a rapidly expanding market for their products. Then, predictably, the general growth of the segment slowed. Dean's business was vulnerable as consolidation became inevitable.

One particular direct report, a VP, knew exactly how to exploit Dean's weaknesses in order to elevate his own position and expand his influence. He convinced Dean to put him in charge of an area of the business that was well outside his expertise. Eventually, this VP influenced Dean to make some decisions that caused considerable damage to the business. In the end, Dean's role was diminished by the board of directors, the business was sold to a competitor, and Dean left the organization after the acquisition was completed.

Real leadership is required

Real leaders of community-based non-profit organizations need much more than technical expertise or an impressive set of academic accomplishments. They also need more than an emotional link to their cause and a strong conviction that they need to do something about it. Many people who hold formal leadership positions in community-based non-profits are simply not qualified to lead. This sounds like a harsh and sweeping statement. Undoubtedly, some people will take issue with it. Leaders in the CBNP segment usually have a profound sense of commitment to their cause, but they frequently lack the qualities, disciplines, and competencies that leaders need. Some of them should never have been permitted to assume a formal leadership role. Some simply defaulted into leadership because they were available to assume a particular job, rather than because an extensive search process located an outstanding candidate.

Many people who hold formal leadership positions in community-based non-profits are simply not qualified to lead.

In the world of CBNPs, there is no shortage of passion and compassion. Who is ultimately responsible for the challenge of inadequate leadership? Should we blame ambitious individuals who have no idea that their desire to expand their influence exceeds their capabilities? Do we blame the people who do not have enough courage to tell them that they lack leadership skills? Can processes be put in place to ensure that organizations that serve the vulnerable are well led? Have the complexities of modern leadership made leading more challenging than it once was? Leadership, by all accounts, is hard, lonely, and often thankless. In a non-profit context, it can be particularly challenging.

As a result of ineffective leadership, a number of people have endured terrible employment experiences after joining the staff of a community-based non-profit. Some people worked in ill-defined roles in poorly managed organizations. They may have felt compelled by an overwhelming passion they felt for a particular cause, but they quickly found themselves jaded or burned out. They assumed that the work environment would be blissful and invigorating. Instead, they found little more than frustration. Some people have taken on roles in CBNPs expecting that they would be surrounded by dedicated, lovely, inspiring people, only to realize that the realities of day-to-day work on the front lines (or behind the scenes) of a non-profit organization can be remarkably similar to any other "job." In almost every organization, there are people with entitlement mentalities, there are needy co-workers, and people who appear to be there for the wrong reasons. Most CBNPs have employees or volunteers who are not fully aligned with the purposes of the organization. There will be "workplace politics" that can distract people from the real work of the organization. Additionally, everywhere, including in all segments of the private sector, there will be inexperienced or incompetent managers. A contributing factor to the paucity of quality leadership is the assumption that since community-based non-profits are chronically underfunded, they cannot find or recruit the best leaders. A CBNP that aims to hire inexpensive management talent will obtain the level of leadership that they pay for. This can contribute to a "we do the best we can even if it is rather sub-standard" mindset and a willingness to make excuses for inadequate leaders.

Leadership is built upon two pillars: CREDIBILITY and RAPPORT.

Leadership is built upon two pillars: CREDIBILITY and RAPPORT. Without these pillars, a leader cannot function. Any observer of leadership might point to politicians as prime examples of the need for both of these pillars. A leader of an organized political party will not survive if she or he lacks credibility and rapport. Sometimes a massive meltdown in one area leads to an inability to marshal enough of the other. George H.W. Bush might have been one of the most qualified men to ever become President of the United States, but he struggled towards the end of his presidency to develop sufficient rapport with ordinary people. This eventually contributed to his electoral defeat in 1992. Conversely, Bill Clinton, who defeated Mr. Bush, was adept at building a high level of rapport with people, but lost a lot of credibility during the scandal that resulted in his impeachment. In Great Britain, Tony Blair enjoyed a high degree of credibility and rapport until a number of regrettable decisions around the time of the invasion of Iraq caused a decline in both.

Credibility is often described as the combination of perceived expertise and trustworthiness that inspires confidence. A credible person is often well qualified, intelligent, skilled, and experienced. Credibility often takes a lot of time to establish, but it can be quickly destroyed. A leader usually gains credibility by taking action that is perceived to be consistent with the words they say or the ideas they espouse. Rapport is a bit different, and is harder to define. It involves the ability to connect quickly with people and to meet them and engage with them on their terms. Some leaders are naturally good at building rapport. They walk into a room and they "own the room." They are naturally friendly and warm. They are approachable and project candour. People who meet them feel as if they have been seen and heard. Rapport-builders can often change the temperature in a room from hostile and suspicious to receptive and calm.

Four typical leadership styles found in community-based non-profits

CBNPs tend to celebrate leaders who are idealistic and self-sacrificing. In some cases, a leader may not actually accomplish a great deal. Instead a leader may be adept at obtaining financing, gaining media attention, or getting nominated for awards. Some are celebrated for financial sacrifices they have made or for health problems they have encountered as a result of their work. Non-profit sector leaders often fall into one of four "types." These types, described below, do not pretend to describe every leadership style. However, it isn't unusual for an outside observer to be able to identify one or more of these in most CBNP leaders.

The Amiable Activist

CBNP organizations that are led by well-intentioned activists can achieve a certain amount of notoriety because the leader is often able to assemble a group of like-minded followers. As a result, Amiable Activists can be influenced by the narrative of the person with whom they last spoke. They seek out affirmation and alignment with their purpose.

They may overlook gaps in talent within their team as long as people are fully signed up to the cause. They project happiness even when they are in a deep crisis.

Organizations that serve vulnerable people need allies, and this style of leader seeks out devotees to the cause and will do their best to develop a network of friends and supporters. This leadership style can be problematic if the leader is so positive that they avoid making hard decisions. If a leader does not like to have difficult conversations or say "no", it merely pushes the problem or confrontation down the road. The leader's instinct may be to strive for harmony and seek peace at all costs. In pursuit of group happiness, the leader may call a meeting to diffuse a disagreement and start by declaring that there is consensus around an issue, when it is clear to everyone that there is nothing that remotely resembles consensus.

Leadership that avoids confrontation or puts an unwarranted premium on surface level harmony may look good to outside observers, but it usually generates frustration inside the organization, particularly if the leader refuses to address internal politics or organizational inefficiencies.

The Charismatic Founder

Many CBNPs are led by a person who had an initial vision for the organization. They may have seen a need and started the operation to try to address the need. Many non-profits do not grow beyond the one-person start-up phase, and this is not necessarily a bad thing. The founder may be addressing an urgent local need and may be able to develop a cohort of volunteers who assist in the cause. The need may stabilize or diminish, and there may be little reason for the operation to grow or expand.

Frequently though, when these operations attempt to grow, they struggle because of an absence of vision and an absence of leadership scope that would require the marshalling of additional resources. Charismatic founders are often deeply driven by a sense of calling and are typically less focused on organizational development and the establishment of effective processes. Founders of organizations, for profit or non-profit, often arrive at a point where their skills do not align with the needs of a growing organization. There are numerous examples in the corporate world where boards have been forced to step in and sideline a founder in order to protect the business. Unfortunately, non-profit boards usually permit long-time founder/leaders to remain in place even though the organization's requirements exceed the leader's capacity.

> Unfortunately, non-profit boards usually permit long-time founder/leaders to remain in place even though the organization's requirements exceed the leader's capacity.

Leaders who lead established organizations for extended periods of time can also fall into this classification. They may not be the founder, but by virtue of leading the organization for 10 to 20 years (sometimes longer), they fall prey to "the curse of the founder." This phenomenon is fairly common in CBNPs that have enjoyed the stability of having the same leader for a long period of time. The organization, over time, becomes synonymous with the leader. Typically, there is a certain amount of organizational atrophy, and a belief develops that the organization could never survive without its leader. The leader feeds that belief or, at least, does nothing to dissuade those who propagate it. If the organization has a weak board, board members will usually allow the leader to remain in place in perpetuity or will allow her/him to select their successor (usually a huge error). Founders, or long-term leaders, need to have a formal succession plan, and the board of the organization needs to ensure that the plan is updated frequently so that the CBNP can continue when a charismatic founder departs.

The Connected Fundraiser

Many CBNPs are led by people who are skilled promoters and rainmakers. They connect easily with celebrities, prominent politicians, and funders. Fundraising is as vital in the non-profit sector as sales and marketing are in the for-profit sector. A leader who is also a talented fundraiser can cover a lot of ground and ensure the financial well-being of the organization. Without the fuel of ongoing funding, it is impossible for any organization to survive.

The challenge of the Connected Fundraiser is that leaders with a strong fundraising focus can develop blind spots around organizational effectiveness. Organizations can stagnate when the leader has a one-dimensional preoccupation with the essentials of fundraising. When donors, fundraising events, promotional campaigns, and developing political connections that lead to government grants or contracts becomes the principal focus of the leader, the effectiveness of the organization can suffer.

The leader of a CBNP usually needs to invest a percentage of their time in a fundraising role. Frequently, this is a significant percentage of a leader's time. Meeting key donors or funding agencies often cannot be delegated. However, when the senior leader of the organization invests most of her/his energy in securing the top line of the organization's income statement, problems in the rest of the organization are seldom addressed promptly. If the organization reaches a certain size, it is likely unhelpful to try to perform the role of Executive Director and Fundraiser simultaneously. A leader needs to pay close attention to important decisions on spending, delivery of programs, human resource management, and operations.

The Somewhat Likeable Grizzly

Several years ago, the Somewhat Likeable Grizzly leadership style was quite prevalent in CBNPs. It is characterized by a moderately caustic, hands-on leader who delivers needed services along with a big dose of tough love to clients. These leaders often become legends, and people tend to love them and overlook their idiosyncrasies and their rough exterior. They are colourful and iconic characters who can quickly become media darlings because journalists are able to obtain controversial quotes or newsworthy interviews. They are never bland or boring and are characterized by an extremely independent spirit. They dislike advice or anything that they perceive as interference. Their personalities and strong convictions drive behaviours that often keep others at a distance. They are respected for what they have accomplished, but they tend to struggle to develop or maintain partnerships. They may even alienate some donors or potential supporters. They tend to exude confidence and be utterly convinced that they, and only they, understand the needs of the clients and the needs of their organization.

This heartfelt sense of being "the only person who truly gets it" guides the leader's management style and, as a result, they tend to burn through team members. In fact, they prefer to cultivate obedient followers, rather than develop working relationships with collaborators. There are numerous examples of CBNPs that have never reached their full potential, mostly because of their leader's inability to engage and retain quality people. The result is that their organizations tend to bounce from one self-inflicted mini-crisis to another. A CBNP typically declines or closes when the Somewhat Likeable Grizzly departs or retires. Many actually die on the job. It is rare to witness a successful transition involving a leader of this type. Typically, transitions are exceedingly painful and destabilizing.

Real leaders are courageous servants

CBNPs need to find and retain real leaders. It is not only about finding people who are in love with the cause or have a set of desirable credentials. It cannot be about power or prestige. A real leader has to be prepared to serve the cause. They are not the cause. Their preferences do not supersede the cause. Often, leaders can only lead an organization up to a point. It takes courage and discernment to know when that point has been reached. Some non-profits need to consider hiring people who have a track record of handling senior level responsibility in settings outside the non-profit sector. When real leaders are leading, it makes a huge difference. Talented leaders elevate the performance of the team and provide the gentle guidance to get the organization to fulfill its potential.

Courageous leadership is like courageous parenting. A courageous parent will not do whatever their toddlers want; they will do what they believe is best for them and the family. Leaders should always listen very carefully and consult broadly, but they should not set vision by consensus or make changes based solely on what team members, clients, or stakeholders say they want. They are sometimes called upon to make difficult decisions and to act with speed and conviction in challenging situations or when faced with adversity.

> A real leader has to be prepared to serve the cause. They are not the cause.

Real leaders develop a strategy that can be implemented

Increasingly, non-profit organizations are becoming clearer in describing their mission and vision. The challenge that most non-profits face is ensuring that there is a shared and agreed-upon strategy. The vision and mission answers the *why* and *what*. Strategy answers the *how*. Once the *how* is determined, the organization needs a strategic implementer who is gifted and equipped to lead and ensure that ideas are translated into actions. Ideas remain dreams unless the dots are connected and there is a credible plan that systematically sets out how to move from the concept to the reality. This includes ensuring that the plans they make are realistic and have logical contingencies in the event that obstacles emerge. The difference between a dreamer and a visionary is implementation.

> The difference between a dreamer and a visionary is implementation.

Real leaders develop resiliency

Flexibility is essential to developing and enriching the resilience of a leader. It means keeping emotions from hijacking good reason, being able to detach oneself in order to step back and gain perspective, and understanding that the past is the past. It also means engaging resources to inform your next choice. In short, the greater the resilience, the greater the chance a leader will avoid burnout.

The role of a leader in any setting is challenging, however leading in a CBNP setting has a few nuances that add complexity. These include the need to be highly nurturing and sympathetic, while also being able to move forward decisively when action is called for. The sector also requires leaders who can build and maintain supportive and positive relationships with a variety of diverse stakeholders.

> Burnout happens when a full plate of non-stop activities produces very few satisfying results.

Leaders who develop resiliency are able to pace themselves so that they operate in a sustainable way. A resilient leader develops vigilance around their daily agenda, identifying the things that are unlikely to add value to their organization, and finding ways to eliminate them. In a non-profit setting, there is a temptation to go to every local committee meeting or accept every speaking invitation. This can result in fatigue or worse, burnout. Burnout usually happens when a full plate of non-stop activities produces very little in the way of satisfying results.

Leaders can develop resiliency by focusing as much energy as they can on a few key things that are the main drivers of success in the organization. They can also develop resiliency by knowing what their unique gifts are and by making sure that as much of their time as possible is invested in using those unique gifts. As important, they need to engage in supportive, pleasing, and nurturing activities outside of the workplace. Though it sounds obvious, every leader needs to relax and carve out downtime. The best leaders typically develop a regular discipline of being immersed in other interests. These could include things like long bike rides, hikes up a mountain, or attending theatre productions.

Real leaders express constructive discontent in productive ways

An outstanding leader will be an effective communicator of the organization's vision and mission. The leader also needs to affirm people who take actions that are fully aligned with the vision and mission. However, it is equally vital for a leader to recognize, with humility, that the organization has not fully reached its aspirations or that there are important challenges ahead. This is often difficult because any encouragement to improve can be perceived as critical or demotivating. Constructive discontent, when it is communicated in tandem with a realistic plan, will illuminate pathways to future success. Nobody likes to hear that what they are doing is less than ideal or get the sense that they have been rowing in circles.

> Courageous leaders will take the initiative to stand up and say, "We can do better, and here is how."

Courageous leaders will take the initiative to stand up and say, "We can do better, and here is how." This can include a personal acknowledgement of a need to change course; something like, "I used to believe that we needed to go in this direction, but now the evidence is clear that there is a better way to arrive at our goals."

Real leaders are unafraid to challenge their organizations to evolve, and are ready to guide the process of change

When leaders introduce change, two things typically happen right away. Firstly, people will feel awkward, ill at ease, and self-conscious because ingrained habits are being disrupted. This tends to make people feel uncomfortable as they struggle to eliminate the old ways of responding. Secondly, people initially focus on what they have to give up or lose, even if they didn't really like it, or it wasn't working. The known always seems safer than the unknown or untried. That is why effective leaders are both proactive and gentle in showing the team that they understand the challenge and discomfort of the change. If the team perceives the leader as emotionally and practically supportive during the tough times, the process of change will be easier.

Leaders need to recognize that people who undergo too much change within too short a time will become dysfunctional, and in some cases may become physically sick. While it is impossible to control every change, it is important to avoid piling change upon change upon change. While changes bring opportunity to do other positive things, the timing of additional changes is important. When a leader contemplates introducing changes, it is often good to test the potential for resistance to the change to determine if the timing is correct. A good question to ask is: "How would you feel if…" Some people thrive on constant change. It is exciting to them. Others do not like change because it is threatening to them. Leaders understand that any change will have supporters and people who have difficulty adapting. In time, most team members who resist initially will come onside. Open discussion and permission to raise concerns can often be the most effective pathway to achieving a major change.

Change takes time and effort, even if it has the long-term effect of improving services or reducing workload. It takes time for people to digest change. It is important for leaders to acknowledge that change won't be instantaneous and ensure that practical support is provided. It is also important to periodically review the necessity of tasks and determine whether they are still essential. If a leader fails to reinforce the change and continually outline the need for it, people will revert to their old behaviours. If people perceive that the leaders are not serious about doing things the new way, they will go back to the old way. Sometimes this will be in the open, and sometimes it will be covert. The leader must remind people that there is a new course, and that the new course will remain. Furthermore, the leader must walk the talk.

Some may assume that the non-profit sector is immune from change because the nature of the work is tied so closely to deep feelings of compassion for those they serve. Compassion is essential, but compassion alone is not the fuel of transformation. Transformation is contingent upon courageous leadership.

> Compassion is essential, but compassion alone is not the fuel of transformation.

Leaders of non-profits must have the courage to set high expectations

Non-profits frequently find themselves under-resourced and, in many cases, they have developed a habit of muddling through. A culture of excuse-making can set in. Statements like "We're only a non-profit…" become self-limiting, energy-depleting mantras. When people in an organization develop and propagate an internal narrative that suggests that they can be second-rate, or when sloppiness is tolerated, the organization can develop plausible excuses that quickly become a rigid framework of perceived limitations. Leaders must have the conviction to break through this kind of thinking or the organization will not be able to progress. They must model excellence and inspire the organization to develop a culture of constant improvement. Additionally, non-profit boards need to attract and retain quality leaders and ensure that they maintain an appropriate equilibrium in the way that they monitor them. This equilibrium ideally balances support and encouragement with suitable checks and balances. CBNP boards that fail to attract, support, and retain talented Executive Directors are often the root cause of stagnation. For any CBNP to move ahead, its board of directors needs to identify the qualities required in the day-to-day leader of the organization and create an environment that allows the leader to thrive and succeed.

CHAPTER 7
Why do many boards of community-based non-profits miss the mark?

Effective governance by a board of trustees is a relatively rare and unnatural act... because the tides of trusteeship carry boards in the wrong direction: from strategy towards operation, from long-term challenges towards immediate concerns, from collective action towards individual initiatives.
—Richard Chait, Thomas Holland, and Barbara Taylor, Improving the Performance of Governing Boards, American Council on Education, 1996

THE PROBLEM: Very few boards in the community-based non-profit sector function effectively, and almost all non-profit boards struggle to attract the right board members with appropriate experience.

In the course of my consulting practice from 2001-2016, I was exposed to a variety of non-profit boards. My observation has been that almost every individual board member was committed to the cause of the organization they were serving, however very few board members had a solid grasp of their role, unless they had obtained formal governance training. To be recognized as an engineer, doctor, lawyer, actuary, or accountant, an individual must have recognized educational and professional credentials. In most cases they are also required to complete ongoing education that updates their understanding of the profession. However, almost anyone, qualified or unqualified, suitable or unsuitable, can be appointed or elected to a board that exists to provide a CBNP with oversight and governance. What could possibly go wrong? Answer: everything!

A Story About a Board Failure

> Prior to joining the non-profit organization where I currently serve, I had the opportunity to work closely on consulting assignments with a number of non-profit organizations. Almost all of this work was pro bono. In almost every case, the scope of my role was to assist the board and the Executive Director of the organization by identifying challenges and establishing workable processes to address gaps in the overall performance

of the organization. Frequently, this started with a need to deal with serious concerns about overall governance and board-related processes.

As one might expect, the initial analysis almost always uncovered a variety of perplexing challenges. Sometimes these challenges were caused directly by the way the organization operated. In many other cases, practices and policies had simply not kept pace with a modest amount of growth in the organization's activities. Sadly, in almost all cases, the principal obstacle to accelerated performance was a dysfunctional volunteer board. Frequently, the problem could be isolated to a minority of board members. The following story is true, but I have changed critical details to mask the identity of the organization.

I walked into the room on a Saturday morning and greeted the two board members who I knew. They had advised me that the board was divided on the need to engage with an outside person to help them build an effective strategy. However, I was going to do this for free, as a favour to one of the board members, so the price was right. Who knows, maybe they got what they paid for that particular Saturday.

The board consisted of five people, all of whom had no experience in governance, but were quite devoted to the cause. In my view, five board members represented the right size for a small non-profit that had begun as a one-person operation, but which was progressing to the point where the one underpaid employee and a handful of volunteers were experiencing substantial organizational challenges. The overall resources were insufficient relative to the organization's needs. This was a classic case of demand/resource imbalance.

My assignment was to help guide the board through a process to produce the very first strategic plan for that organization. My method for arriving at a strategic plan has always been to ask the leadership to distil an organization's vision, mission, and core values. With these established, prior to the start of a strategic planning session, we typically evaluate a SWOT analysis (Strengths, Weaknesses, Opportunities, Threats) that the Executive Director has prepared. We review it to test its validity. The next step is to assess strategic alternatives that flow from the opportunities or threats that are identified using a few questions that I supply to participants.

This is normally an easy enough process for a three to four-hour strategic session and, with some guidance, it always leads to a series of next steps, if it is well facilitated. I had facilitated many similar sessions, and this one looked like it could be rather easy. The board members had all completed their pre-work and submitted it. The number of viable strategic options looked to be fairly limited; something that is not uncommon with small CBNPs that function in a limited geographical area.

On this particular Saturday morning it did not go well. The initial discussion led us to expose a series of unspoken misunderstandings and misconceptions that had existed for a long time in the organization. The five board members had five completely different perspectives on the challenges that the organization was facing. This created five divergent ideas about what the next steps ought to be. None of the five board members had any particular expertise related to strategy, and when we began to review strategic alternatives, they did a deep dive into the operational mechanics of the organization. This is a normal challenge in strategic planning.

An experienced facilitator often has to steer the discussion away from tactics and back towards identifying strategies. In this case, it was particularly painful to see a couple of board members dismiss a particular strategic imperative outright because of some perceived operational limitations. Ironically, their operational concerns would have been addressed by adoption of the strategy in question. In other words, the board members could not get their mind around the future. They were stuck in a rut, framing everything in the context of the past and the present.

Unlike some board meetings that I have attended, there was no acrimony or hostility. I did not see any eye-rolling or negative non-verbal cues. Nobody stormed out of the meeting. Smiles were exchanged and the dialogue was incredibly pleasant. The board members simply talked past each other in annoyingly polite ways. Several of them were clearly not equipped to be board members. I can remember wondering to myself if there was any chance that this organization, which was trying to do meaningful work in the community, would survive this board. The meeting ended without any specific action plan, and the little non-profit has continued to soldier on valiantly.

I wish that this Saturday morning session could have been helpful, but I fear it was a waste of time for everyone.

While this story illustrates one of the dysfunctions that I have observed in CBNP boards, it is far from the most damaging. When a volunteer board is little more than a collection of willing individuals who have a limited grasp of the principles of governance, the organization typically is unable to advance, and the people who are tasked to do the day-to-day work do not benefit from the steady guidance and strategic orientation that a board ought to provide. If this were a company that was marketing products or services, it would be unfortunate, but when it is an organization that is delivering important services to vulnerable people in the community, the lost opportunity to do the right things in the right way is tragic. Ultimately, those who suffer are those who need the organization the most, its clients.

> Boards that are either benignly unhelpful or mildly dysfunctional will impede or delay progress.

Virtually every CBNP operates with a volunteer board. Having an "arm's-length non-remunerated board" is a typical requirement for obtaining official recognition and charitable status. A board in a non-profit ought to provide perceived stability and ensure that there is effective financial oversight. The challenge is that they are often part of the reason why organizations struggle to move forward. Most volunteer boards tend to accomplish very little and can easily become dysfunctional. Independent observers report that most non-profit boards meet regularly, but merely go through the motions of governance. Some boards waste a lot of energy on unwise operational debates or political infighting, and do little to advance the cause they claim to espouse. A diverse collection of well-meaning volunteers is seldom ipso facto equipped to deliver the kind of oversight that a board needs to provide. Boards that are either benignly unhelpful or mildly dysfunctional will impede or delay progress.

> Should governance be exercised by trained, professional board members who are paid?

This raises an important issue. Should we reconsider the assumption that a community-based non-profit organization needs to be governed by a **volunteer** board? Instead, should governance be exercised by trained, professional board members who might even be remunerated? It is important to stress that non-profits ought to have a governance structure that ensures appropriate accountability. They cannot simply operate based on the whims of an Executive Director or CEO, no matter how capable or enlightened that CEO may be. Furthermore, any leader needs to have the "cover of accountability."

Attracting the right, or the wrong, board members

Often, the individuals who are attracted to becoming board members are people who are accustomed to taking action. They may have problem-solving reflexes, or they may specialize in providing rapid assessments of challenges, coupled with detailed prescriptions to solve it. They frequently have impressive professional credentials or a resume that highlights important accomplishments.

The challenge with accomplished, action-oriented people is that the experience they bring may not have prepared them for the exercise of governance in the context of a CBNP. They are usually accustomed to being the experts in the room on a specific matter like finance, communication, or medical services. Instead, in their capacity as a board member, they may have to recognize that the exercise of governance involves asking questions, validating responses, and providing suggestions rather than directives. Board members who flaunt their expertise or flex their muscles, based on a perception that they are "where the buck stops," misunderstand the fundamentals of governance.

A board exists to ensure that the CBNP stays focused on its mandate, acts in ways that are transparent, and takes appropriate measures to mitigate risks. Board members sometimes struggle with this because it is easier to provide directives and quote from their professional experience than to ask helpful and relevant questions. It is far easier to delve into the details of operations, programs, human resources, or finances. It is even easier to waste valuable time in board meetings on issues that add no value to the cause.

> A board exists to ensure that the CBNP stays focused on its mandate, acts in ways that are transparent, and takes appropriate measures to mitigate risks.

The structure and content of an agenda for a board meeting will often determine the outcome of the board meeting. When an agenda isn't sharp, short, and focused, the board meeting will be chaotic.

Agendas are important, but people determine how the agenda is managed. Unfortunately, many boards have at least one member who is either temperamentally unfit or thoroughly unqualified to be a board member. These situations are rarely addressed, because nobody wants to deal with them. It is never easy to have a hard conversation with someone who is disruptive or unqualified. The person in question is usually blissfully unaware that they are not providing valuable service to the organization, and they often lack sufficient emotional intelligence to notice that others are tiptoeing around them.

A "slightly rogue" board member is usually able to exert undue influence, hijack the agenda, or systematically frustrate other board members. There are many examples of boards that make little progress due to a "Belligerent Bob," "Overbearing Oliver," or "Negative Nellie." Unfortunately, it is quite normal for CBNP boards to have a least one member who might be defined as either "needy" or "toxic." Their behaviours run the range from emotion-laced outbursts to passive-aggressive posturing. They see no problem with delivering authoritative or challenging statements that are punctuated by inferences they can later claim were unintended. Many times, there is a joy-killing overtone in their remarks. They take themselves too seriously. They may not be fun people, and they want to make sure that nobody else is having fun either. Alternatively, they are blissfully unaware of their impact on other people. I have had the opportunity to observe board meetings where most of the time and energy was devoted to managing the participation of people who should never have been invited to be board members. In other instances, the presence of ill-equipped people results in protracted discussion on issues that do not warrant the attention of the group of people assembled.

> Whenever there are problems in a volunteer board, there is usually a corresponding absence of understanding of the purpose and role of the board.

Whenever there are problems in a volunteer board, there is usually a corresponding absence of understanding of the purpose and role of the board. Other dysfunctions range from major personality conflicts to legitimate and persistent differences in vision for the organization. More often than not, there are also significant differences in perceptions arising out of board deliberations. The additional difficulty is that the collective memory of a board is unreliable, even with the benefit of the minutes of past meetings. Time and energy can be lost trying to contextualize things that happened a year or two ago.

Putting the focus on governance

A number of scholarly articles and books have been written about governance in recent years and specific directives related to the essentials of board governance. These articles and books are easy to obtain and can provide far more insight than this chapter will provide, but effective governance is fundamental to the reform needed in CBNPs. To put it succinctly, ineffective volunteer boards are a major contributor to the challenges and misdiagnosed shortcomings of community-based non-profit organizations. For change to happen in any organization, it needs to include the board. Sometimes it needs to start with the board.

> For change to happen in any organization, it needs to include the board. Sometimes it needs to start with the board.

A CBNP ought to clearly define and articulate core principles of governance in a formal board manual. However, a really good board manual isn't the solution. Sometimes the perceived guardians of the organization's governance are legalistic or process-oriented board members who are focused on rigidly following their personal interpretation of the organization's manual and bylaws or who slavishly adhere to Robert's Rules of Order in meetings. Running a tight meeting and following processes is not synonymous with effective governance. Boards that equate success with the micromanagement of their meetings do so because that is the default position of the people who aren't properly equipped to serve on a board. When people are unclear on the scope of their responsibilities, it always feels good to follow a set of rules or historically accepted procedures.

Another mistake that some CBNP board members make is to involve themselves in the operational details of the organization. One Executive Director recounted a story about a situation he uncovered when he was first appointed. At each board meeting, the entire senior staff was required to deliver activity reports, and board members provided detailed feedback and developmental input to them. Needless to say, the new Executive Director put a stop to that practice. A board must work with, and through, the leader of the organization, usually the Executive Director. There is nothing wrong with board members engaging in informal dialogue with staff members of the organization; however, the purpose of a meeting of the board of directors should not include listening to staff reports or providing guidance to the organization's employees. The board has one employee – the CEO or other designated leader of the organization.

> Board meetings should be focused exclusively on two types of information—decision information and monitoring information.

John Carver, a recognized expert in governance, has stated that board meetings should be focused exclusively on two types of information. They are decision information and monitoring information. In his view, decision information is prospective, and it contains data or facts that will lead to a decision that the board is required to make, such as the establishment of budget parameters. Monitoring information, on the other hand, is often misunderstood or interpreted as the need to know everything. In fact monitoring information should consist of systematic verification of pre-established criteria. If the board sets out ratios or performance targets, then it needs to check to see if performance is tracking in the right direction. This information is both current and retrospective. An example might be that overall expenses are limited to a defined level in each quarter. If this sort of goal is established, then the board needs to check to make sure that it is happening.

It is very important for a board to realize that the only time it acts as a board is when it meets together in a board meeting. Outside the framework of a formal board meeting, the board is merely a collection of interested individuals. It is therefore critical that board meetings be well planned and focused on the essential matters of governance. Board meetings that stray from issues of governance are, at best, ineffective, and at worst, a train wreck. Some board meetings waste valuable time and energy on comparative assessments of existing programs or spend time debating issues that very few of the people around the table understand. An effective board ought to spend the majority of its time looking at where the CBNP needs to go. They should not allow operational issues to make their way onto the agenda. They should also resist conducting extensive post-mortems or second-guessing program-related decisions.

> Some board meetings waste valuable time and energy on comparative assessments of existing programs or spend time debating issues that very few of the people around the table understand.

It is the board's primary responsibility to hire the day-to-day leader for the organization and then provide her or him with a definition of success. This can take the form of measurable short and longer-term objectives or an agreed upon set of operating imperatives. A CBNP that is equipped to function properly needs a board that can ask the right questions and provide the right kind of support to the leader of the organization. When a qualified leader is in place, the board needs to be a group of cheerleaders for the organization and act as trusted advisors for the leader, while staying out of the way of day-to-day operations. One of the most critical relationships in the organization is the relationship between the board and the CEO or most senior day-to-day leader. The relationship, according to most experts, works best when it is collegial rather than hierarchical. Sadly, the evidence suggests that the number one reason for the departure of excellent leaders from community-based non-profits is due to conflict or frustration with the board.

> The evidence suggests that the number one reason for the departure of excellent leaders from community-based non-profits is due to conflict or frustration with the board.

What does the board need to know and do?

A board must know what risks exist in the operating environment, and they need to ensure that management has taken appropriate measures to mitigate the risks. It is also the board's job to ensure that the core objectives of the CBNP remain front and centre, and that the organization is appropriately resourced and equipped to accomplish its mission. A board that does not understand its role will always find things to tinker with or meddle in. Board members that see themselves as owners of the non-profit typically begin to act in ways that are detrimental to the organization they are meant to be serving.

The board of a for-profit business is mandated to represent the shareholders of that business. Their actions and decisions are expected to reflect the interests of the shareholders. While it is important for the board of a business to consider the entire ecosystem within which the business exists, the primary issue in any decision will be the risk and reward factors for those who are monetarily invested in the enterprise. A CBNP is slightly different. Very few CBNPs operate to satisfy the objectives of investors, but they always have stakeholders. These interested parties may include donors, partners, government officials, clients, and volunteers. Stakeholders have diverse expectations, but are usually united by a commitment to a cause, even though they may have different definitions of the cause. Therefore, the board of a CBNP must be the guardian of the fundamental purpose of the organization, with a careful eye on the needs and aspirations of all the stakeholders who are engaged in that purpose.

> The board of a CBNP must be the guardian of the fundamental purpose of the organization, with a careful eye on the needs and aspirations of all the stakeholders who are engaged in that purpose. A board that does not understand its role will always find things to tinker with or meddle in.

Good governance includes setting written guidelines around what a board really needs to focus on. The board of a CBNP should be ensuring that the major initiatives of the organization are coherently aligned with its cause and mission. This can be measured, to some extent, by having a few big picture goals or objectives that are within the control of the Executive Director. However, it is equally important that any review of these objectives, or accountability related to them, focus on the trajectory rather than the outcome. In some cases, time-bound objectives can be elusive in the context of the community service sector since funding may be fluid and because a non-profit organization cannot dictate the actions of clients or key partners.

As an example, an organization may aim to help 40 women escape violent relationships and obtain secure housing each year. At the end of the year, the organization may have only assisted 21 women, but this may not be a missed goal. The difference in the numbers could be due to the timing of available housing, challenges with program funding, or a reduction in the number of women experiencing violence in that community. In this case, a board-level evaluation should ask for information about the trends and not focus on the timeline of the objective.

Limited time and limited understanding

On average, a board member of a non-profit will spend between 18 and 28 hours per year in board meetings, including the preparation for such board meetings. This is not enough time for anyone to get a good grasp of every issue that the staff or volunteers are dealing with, day in and day out. Board members also have to deal with many different issues in their own professional endeavours. Some are active professionals who may be involved in many different causes or may sit on a variety of boards. Board members who think that they have to understand all of the issues of the CBNP badly misunderstand the purpose of board governance. They may not be the kind of people who should be invited to join a board.

> Board members cannot be fully immersed in the day-to-day details of the organization and are simply not in a position to make some decisions.

Board members cannot be fully immersed in the day-to-day details of the organization and are simply not in a position to make some decisions. Yet, often, a board deliberately meanders into a discussion that leads to a decision even though many board members are not sufficiently able to appreciate the nuances that must be factored in. This can become extremely demotivating for board members, and it will frustrate the senior staff of the organization. Ultimately, a volunteer board member will wonder why she/he is investing valuable time in meetings that feature circular discussions or deep dives into operational details that are hard to grasp.

The question might be asked: How can key operational details be shared in a way that allows board members to be conversant with the issues facing the organization? There are lots of simple informal processes. One way is to have management provide a series of regular, brief written updates that supply the board members with tidbits of news and information. This process can serve the needs of the board while avoiding the tendency to confuse it with governance. This can also occur by including board members in the circulation of internal newsletters or by sending the board a brief message from time to time that summarizes events and milestones.

Operational updates should not be part of the agenda of any board meeting unless the CBNP is so small that the board is actually operating the organization. However, if the board, or some board members, are running the day-to-day operations of the organization, the number one agenda item probably should be to design a process that will put an end to that. Typically, when a board invests time discussing the details of day-to-day operations one of two things occur, and neither is good.

1. The board is inclined to try to direct specific tactics and can become far too involved in things that are the purview of the staff. This is a common error in smaller CBNPs because the board is more likely to be aware of small details or feel a need to control certain types of spending. A board that takes the time to review every expenditure related to a minor renovation project in a building is not governing. It is micromanaging. It is always possible that the cost of a project is an important financial issue; however, it is usually far more productive to have the Treasurer review the details in advance of the board meeting and then submit a summary to the board so that the discussion can be limited. A board full of people who were not involved in the details of a renovation project will not add much value to a discussion about what did or did not happen. Furthermore, a group of people who are not fully informed about a specific topic are ill advised to invest meeting time trying to get to the bottom of it.

2. The board invests time digging into multi-dimensional issues that cannot be thoroughly reviewed or understood in a 20 to 30-minute discussion. This results in a process that someone once called "pooling your ignorance." It is particularly dangerous because it is the exact opposite of employing "collective wisdom." A board meeting can derail quickly if the Chair allows extensive discussions on complex issues that are within management's exercise of control. This can produce convoluted concerns that paralyze the decision-making process, even though very few board members may be well versed in the issue. In the face of confusion, a board will usually assume that there is a problem and ask for a more extensive evaluation. The typical outcome is that a board meeting can invest hours going in circles, and the organization can be prevented from moving forward on rather trivial issues.

Should board members be fundraisers?

Board members of CBNP boards can become involved in specific aspects of fundraising. In fact, some boards seem to exist primarily to promote and sell tickets to events that are designed to raise money. In many cases, board members are selected because they can rally a community of wealthy contacts and friends to attend fundraisers. These boards talk about the upcoming fundraising event and may even operate more like a group of event planners than a group that provides governance and guidance. In the case of smaller CBNPs, this can serve the needs of the organization reasonably well in the short term. However, if the board's only focus is the next big event or campaign, the organization itself is usually not well served because board members will see themselves as ticket sellers.

It is perfectly appropriate to encourage board members to be active promoters of the non-profit. After all, why would someone serve on a board if they are not captivated by the cause and the vision of the organization? However, when board members become responsible for most of the fundraising, it creates serious challenges for the organization. First, very few board members are professional fundraisers, and therefore, it's difficult to predict the results that can be anticipated. Second, board members may seek to influence the use of funds that they raise, and this can create a number of unfortunate governance challenges. Third, the efforts of board members may not be aligned with specific fundraising campaigns being led by the internal fundraising team of the organization. When that happens, it can generate confusion in the donor community. Finally, when board members are active fundraisers, the organization itself becomes overly reliant on the ability of individual board members to generate revenues and becomes vulnerable to revenue decreases as board members come and go.

> Challenges in boards are frequently directly attributable to the composition of the board and the culture of the board.

The question of board members as fundraisers elevates another concern about boards that typically exists in the CBNP space. Their struggles and challenges often arise from issues that range from the existence of unqualified but passionate board members to highly qualified but utterly disinterested board members. Challenges in boards are seldom due to the complexity of the bylaws or a poorly written board manual. They are frequently directly attributable to the composition of the board coupled with the culture of the board. The overall culture of the boards of most community organizations is largely determined by the process used to recruit board members. Listed below are some typical descriptions of the composition of many CBNP boards. These descriptions are not exhaustive, nor do they intend to identify an ideal process for the recruitment of a volunteer board. They simply identify how a particular group dynamic might succeed or struggle given its predisposition.

Different types of boards

If an outside observer sought to characterize the composition of the typical boards that exist within the CBNP community in North America, they might find some of the board-types listed below. In some cases, a board might have features of several different types described and therefore have multiple strengths and/or weaknesses.

The Activist Board

Definition: A board that is primarily composed of people who are politically and socially active in promoting a specific cause

Example: A board where all board members are housing rights advocates or a board of dedicated environmental activists

Strength: Board members come to their role with a very strong commitment to the purpose or goal of the organization and, frequently, a set of strong beliefs that favour strong focus on the cause.

Weakness: The board may focus primarily on strategies and tactics to promote the cause, rather than guiding and governing the organization that exists to address the cause.

The Affinity Board

Definition: A board composed of people who are similar or have defining personal characteristics that render them eligible for service on that particular board

Example: A board that requires its members to be of a specific religion, political perspective, or ethnicity

Strength: Board members share a background or heritage that informs their beliefs and actions, and they can have a common, sometimes unspoken, orientation on matters of organizational culture or organizational beliefs.

Weakness: The organization is frequently not able to attract the most effective board members due to a need to conduct a "test of beliefs," "test of political leanings," or "test of heritage." Board conflicts can arise when insignificant issues generate conflicts around individual board members' cultural, political, or belief-related differences, some of which may be unrelated to the purpose or goals of the organization.

The "Lived Experience" Board

Definition: A board composed of people who have been personally affected by the cause

Example: A board full of parents of cancer patients, or a board composed primarily of people who struggle with drug addiction

Strength: Board members share a strong personal connection to the raison d'être of the organization, each having experienced challenges related to the goals of the organization.

Weakness: A strong personal connection to a cause does not automatically make an individual an expert in research, rehabilitation, finance, or governance.

The Prestige Board

Definition: A board composed of famous or well-credentialed people who participate, in part, because their name recognition elevates the visibility of the non-profit

Example: A board that is dominated by high-profile members of a particular community, former politicians, C-suite executives, associates from name brand law firms, or well-known philanthropists

Strength: An organization that can attract very successful people may be able to access high-level contacts and obtain the financial participation of their friends who, in turn, solicit the participation of other well-positioned people or those with considerable expertise.

Weakness: Successful people may not be able to set aside personal preferences in order to achieve board consensus and may disengage when decisions do not align with their views. They may also participate unevenly and may have lower levels of commitment due to scheduling issues.

The Friends of the Executive Director Board

Definition: A board composed of people who are appointed because they have a connection to the day-to-day leader or the founder of the organization

Example: A board that includes a member of the Executive Director's pickup basketball team, her first cousin, her real estate agent, and the owner of the deli across the street

Strength: Board members typically agree with the goals of the leader of the organization and board meetings can be informal and quick.

Weakness: Board members are frequently unqualified for their role and are likely to rubber stamp the proposals of the Executive Director. Conversely, should a serious crisis or conflict occur, these boards are usually ill equipped to deal with it and are likely to unravel quickly, damaging the organization.

The "Occupation Category" Board

Definition: A board composed of people who are selected due to specific, diverse academic credentials or business experience. Some organizations even designate a certain number of board seats for certain kinds of board members (e.g., three board members must be professional engineers)

Example: A board that deliberately and systematically recruits candidates from a list of desired professionals (e.g., a lawyer, an accountant, an academic, an engineer, a medical doctor, and a successful business person)

Strength: The board can claim that it is diverse with respect to skill sets and can call upon the specific education, capabilities or competencies of individual board members for advice.

Weakness: Board members may not be the best possible representatives of their professions and may struggle to function cohesively; because each member is selected due to the kind of work they perform, they may act as subject matter experts who are not inclined to see the big picture.

The Operating Board

Definition: A board composed of people who are heavily invested in the fine details of the day-to-day management of the organization

Example: A group of the most committed volunteers, many of whom regularly perform operational roles in the organization

Strength: Board members tend to have a decent grasp of the day-to-day details and are moderately aware of the ongoing challenges and needs of the organization.

Weakness: Board members typically lack sufficient distance to have an independent perspective on the true weaknesses of the organization. They are usually consumed with small operational details or client needs, and are disinclined to focus on long-term strategy or the disciplines and practices of governance.

Identifying symptoms of dysfunctionality

The ingredients for dysfunction of a CBNP board are often ignored by well-meaning board members in the interest of not rocking the boat. Many boards will conduct cursory self-assessments of their performance, and these can sometimes be a bit self-congratulatory. Boards are usually unable to be candid enough to identify serious collective challenges and decide that they need to be addressed. After all, board members of CBNPs are composed of generous volunteers who are freely devoting their time and talents. This is why it can be helpful to obtain the counsel of an outside observer with proven expertise in governance. An expert in governance will typically look for any of the following five symptoms in order to assess the potential for a problem. Any of these five symptoms are like tremors near an active volcano. They do not predict an eruption or the severity of the damage from an eruption, but they indicate that an eruption is possible.

Symptom 1: Evidence of Disconnected Board Members

When individual board members do not regularly participate in meetings, show up for important events, or get involved in donating time and money to the CBNP, it is a signal that there is a problem. When this is tolerated or excused, it becomes normal behaviour. Board members ought to ensure that they are fulfilling their duties, but they also ought to be observably devoted to the cause of the organization. They should be capable of acting as ambassadors who can coherently articulate the key elements of the vision of the organization. Most board member should also be able to provide a few key examples of how that vision is being operationalized. When board members are not passionate about the cause or do not invest energy to grasp the major components of an organization's main thrust, they should simply move on.

Symptom 2: Board Inertia on Matters of Importance

Decisions need to be made at board meetings. Boards that fail to set out a coherent course of action or arrive at a conclusion on important issues are setting themselves up for calamity. Some boards consistently push weighty matters to future meetings. They may allege that they do not have enough information to reach a decision. There are valid reasons to delay some important decisions but this should be an exception rather than a habit. When an important decision is delayed, the board should ensure that discussions and views are captured in writing so that time is not wasted trying to remember details of past deliberations. Additionally, a time-bound process should be set out to lead towards a decision point.

Symptom 3: An Executive Director Who Has Lost Confidence in the Board

It isn't unusual for discussions among non-profit Executive Directors to include hair-raising stories about the challenges they face with their boards. Building trust and maintaining a strong relationship with a board isn't always easy. An Executive Director has to feel as if the board "has their back." However, it is interesting to observe that the turnover of most Executive Directors is preceded by a loss of trust or confidence. When the day-to-day leader of a CBNP reaches a point of serious frustration with their board, it can be catastrophic for the organization. The effectiveness of many community-based non-profits has been negatively impacted when the Executive Director decides that dealing with their board is draining them of the energy they need to deploy to address the cause of the organization. This is entirely preventable if the Board Chair proactively develops a strong working relationship with the Executive Director that includes regular, candid discussions designed to unearth any concerns or negative feelings that are brewing. Far too many organizations lose quality Executive Directors because of unresolved issues that could have been dealt with before they resulted in a loss of trust.

> The effectiveness of many community-based non-profits has been negatively impacted when the Executive Director decides that dealing with their board is draining them of the energy they need to deploy to address the cause of the organization.

Symptom 4: Unresolved Board Conflict

Boards will always have to manage conflicting views and conflicting approaches. Unanimity of perspective is not possible or desirable. Furthermore, there may be occasional sharp disagreements. If these challenges devolve into personality clashes or disrespect, then they have the potential to become "the issue" of focus. Placating angry board members can become an unwritten element of every board meeting's agenda. Board members must be respectful with each other, but respect includes having hard conversations that seek to honestly put issues on the table and to conclusively resolve them. This does not mean that serious issues should be shoved to one side so that the meeting can move forward. These conversations, for the most part, need to occur in a timely manner. Conflict that is left to simmer tends to grow. This is an area where a Board Chair can act as a mediator outside the board meeting to build trust or confront misperceptions.

Symptom 5: Interference in the Operation of the CBNP by Board Members

Interference can include subtleties like informal or back channel communications between board members and clients, volunteers, partners, or staff. This is extremely damaging even when it is done with allegedly good intentions. Board members of CBNPs often assume that they can wander around in the organization extracting updates and offering advice or wisdom. Some board members may have personal friendships or connections with various stakeholders of the organization, and they may be privy to off-the-record discussions. Board members simply cannot involve themselves in these conversations. They may have to stop someone in mid-sentence and say that they cannot continue to listen. It is possible for board members to create a perception that they are ready or willing to help resolve issues that they simply cannot entertain. A board member may wonder what to do with a complaint that arrives in their email inbox. The best response is to redirect the complainant to the person who is appropriately positioned within the CBNP to deal with their concern.

What should CBNP boards focus on?

Non-profit performance encompasses four concrete areas of interest: financial performance (e.g., donations raised in a year, state funding); stakeholder performance (e.g., volunteer satisfaction, donor loyalty, stakeholder identification); market performance (e.g., non-profit image, non-profit brand reputation, service quality), and mission performance (achieving the mission of the organization). (Mihaltan et al, 2015, 369)

Board discussions need to focus on the elements described above. A solid board will establish a few key indicators that evaluate progress towards the achievement of the strategic intent of the organization. Unless the organization is in a crisis, very little time should be invested by the board in reviewing issues that occurred in the past. Boards that spend time dissecting historical issues are not able to spend enough time considering current and future concerns or opportunities.

Some will ask: Doesn't governance include monitoring the ongoing financial performance of the organization? The answer is a resounding "yes." However, it is unwise to devote more than a few minutes of meeting time to reviewing finances with the obvious exception of annual budget approval, and the review of year-end audited financial statements. Ongoing financial indicators ought to be reviewed in depth by a board-appointed Treasurer, and a summary of key points should be sent to all the directors prior to a board meeting. Organizations that have a reasonably complex financial structure can establish a finance sub-committee composed of board members with financial expertise and members of management to review finances prior to a board meeting. This sub-committee can present the main points in summary form at a board meeting. This prevents circular discussions of financial matters in meetings of the full board where, typically, board members are not expected to be experts in finance or accounting.

When appropriate indicators or metrics of measurement are established, the board can ensure that it is primarily paying attention to the key indicators of progress. To ensure good governance, the organization's Executive Director or CEO should send out brief updates that outline progress, or lack thereof, prior to each board meeting so that board members can ask questions for clarification if there are elements that require additional explanation. Board members should prepare for meetings by reading these updates.

> The transformation of community-based non-profits must include important changes in the approach to board selection and governance.

The transformation of community-based non-profits must include important changes in the approach to board selection and governance. Currently, a non-profit can set itself up with very few restrictions in relation to board composition or member qualifications. The major constraints are those imposed by the organization's by-laws or its board manual—documents that typically prescribe the number of board members, the frequency of board meetings, and the roles of officers. Many organizations develop procedures for how the board operates, and some of the "rules" have become traditions that are not written down anywhere. These can be helpful as touchstones of practice. Sometimes these unwritten things are hard to explain or justify to newer board members. Board members are also frequently unclear about what they need to review and/or approve, versus what they can simply receive as a formal undertaking from management. They may ask about some of these things and receive the response, "We've always done it this way."

The role of the Board Chair is pivotal in orienting a board and framing issues. The role of the Chair includes the overall management and flow of board meetings. The Chair has the responsibility of steering the agenda and guiding discussions to prevent them from wandering into minutia or becoming derailed. However, the Board Chair also has responsibilities outside the board meeting. Knowing what to include and not include in an agenda of a board meeting is often the purview of the Board Chair, in consultation with the Executive Director.

If a well-respected Board Chair has sufficient currency, she or he can also invite ineffective or disruptive board members to reconsider their membership. Recruiting well-qualified and suitable board members is always a challenge, but disinviting current board members can be an even greater challenge, unless it is accomplished with tact and a gracious spirit.

The board needs to provide the organization's leader with appropriate cover for larger decisions. It may also supply some sense of security to major funders, however this sense of security is frequently exaggerated. The stability of many legacy CBNPs is typically linked to the long-term vision and the effectiveness of the senior leader, rather than the stability of a board. Boards usually experience a fair amount of turnover. A board member may serve behind the scenes for three to five years, whereas the Executive Director is typically the very visible day-to-day face of the organization.

Any board model comes with risks. Some boards are hybrids of the composition models described on the previous pages. Unless well-qualified people sit on the boards, none of these models work particularly well. Most boards will muddle through and experience regular turnover of board members. Some ineffective boards invest valuable time debating processes during their formal meetings, while discussing very little in terms of governance and oversight. Anyone who has been part of a dysfunctional board has likely had the dubious privilege of sitting through a meeting that lasted three hours, but accomplished little of substance.

Most CBNP boards make valiant attempts to be as effective as they can be, but often they are unable to envision what effectiveness looks like. Where there are personality clashes, the normal outcome is a departure or series of departures. Well-meaning volunteer board members don't seek to invest time and energy in board meetings only to reap a harvest of frustration. Their motives for serving on a board are often pure, but that does not mean that the outcomes of their service will be optimal. It also does not automatically follow that willingness to serve means that a person is also competent to serve as a board member.

In fairness, there are moderately effective boards that appear to get the job done without self-destructing. The question might be asked: Does that make the model optimal? Or does a particular board work well because the people on the board make it work, despite the limitations of the model?

There is little doubt that talented management coupled with relative financial stability can transcend the challenges of ineffective systems of board governance. The problem is that no board can always count on financial stability in a non-profit setting, nor can it assume that a group of talented managers will be unaffected by problems at the board level. The fact that there are exceptional circumstances and exceptional people is not a reason to maintain a poor system.

> The fact that there are exceptional circumstances and exceptional people is not a reason to maintain a poor system.

Some may ask whether having a less than adequate board or a board that does not know how to exercise governance elevates the risk of failure for a non-profit. The answer is not entirely clear. Some organizations do very well despite a less than ideal or disorganized board. However, more often than not, the dysfunctional nature of the volunteer board contributes to organizational blind spots. This usually leads to a CBNP that is unable to move forward in an effective manner.

A path forward for the CBNP board

Unless there is an impending threat to the existence of the organization, it is wise to orient the focus of community-based non-profit boards around seven principal questions:

1. Is the current financial trajectory aligned with the expectations set out in the approved budget?

2. What actions are being taken to mobilize the organization towards the stated vision?

3. Are there any emerging realities that might have a material impact on the strategy of the organization?

4. Is the organization able to allocate sufficient resources to effectively address the priorities that have been established?

5. Are the people in the organization (employees, volunteers, clients) being well treated and appropriately protected from harm?

6. Is the Executive Director or CEO being provided with the right level of support and encouragement?

7. Are there any potential risks or challenges that could have an impact on the organization and are they being managed appropriately?

The quality of a CBNP's governance will always be influenced by the people who have been recruited to be board members. Typically, boards approach recruitment by appointing a sub-committee to "nominate" potential board members. This committee, if one exists, needs to function with a carefully constructed competency assessment toolkit that allows for an assessment of the style and fit of potential members. The emerging trend that emphasizes the importance of the diversity of board members does not guarantee that the board will function as a board ought to function. Diversity has little to do with competence. Diversity can be defined as diversity of experience or expertise, but the word "diversity" in our current discourse is usually associated with gender and cultural diversity. Having a culturally diverse board may be important, but a board will not suddenly begin to operate well just because there are board members that represent visible minorities or there is age and gender diversity. In fact, diversity can elevate many of the challenges of effective communication.

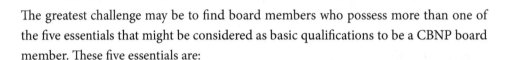

Diversity has little to do with competence. A board will not suddenly begin to operate well when it becomes diverse.

The greatest challenge may be to find board members who possess more than one of the five essentials that might be considered as basic qualifications to be a CBNP board member. These five essentials are:

- **Senior level leadership experience** – A CBNP board needs to attract people who can think like leaders think. A board that is dominated by people who have never led anything will seldom understand the nuances of leadership.

- **Financial understanding** – A board needs people who can quickly grasp basic financial issues and understand financial statements. This doesn't mean that they should be accountants or financial experts. Larger CBNPs ought to have some board members who have professional credentials related to finance or accounting. But all board members should have enough financial literacy to be able to understand a basic set of financial statements.

- **Marketing or public relations skills** – A board needs people who have experience in the subtle art of influence. This kind of experience is useful in the boardroom, and it is also valuable in the exercise of good governance. Board members need to reflect on how their decisions might appear to stakeholders who won't have the benefit of all the information. Board members have to recognize that optics often affect the donor community, and therefore potential perceptions related to the organization must be considered.

- **Curiosity coupled with an ability to learn** – Board members are often selected for their credentials or their connections. They are often evaluated by what they represent or what they know or have accomplished. In a world that is changing rapidly, it is increasingly vital to be able to learn quickly. Board members need to be infused by curiosity and interested in new ideas, new technologies, or new ways of doing things.

- **A well-rounded (not one-dimensional) understanding of the community of clients and stakeholders being served by the organization** – It is important to have a passion for the cause, but it must be anchored in an understanding of the people the organization is serving. It is also important to have, or be able to quickly acquire, a grasp of the overall working environment within which the organization functions.

When a prospective board member has none of these essentials, they are usually ineffective. When they only have one of the five, they are, at best, a subject matter expert. A subject matter expert is of limited value to the process of governance because the expert risks relating to multi-faceted issues through the lens of their own narrow area of expertise. The accountant risks seeing everything as a financial issue that produces revenue or adds expenses. The lawyer may only see dangerous legal risks in all front-line activities. The engineer can push the organization to introduce processes that might be inappropriate for a small project. The community-oriented person may take positions on issues by focusing strictly on the perceived needs of clients. An entrepreneur may want to move quickly on a project and might be comfortable taking chances without assessing the ripple effect of a decision or the future challenges that it might create.

It is not easy to recruit well-rounded people. Still, a CBNP cannot move forward with confidence if it is constrained by a board that majors on minors or delays decisions because the members collectively lack the ability to grasp the fundamentals of the issues they are called upon to address.

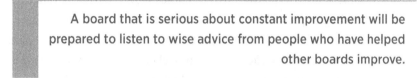

> A board that is serious about constant improvement will be prepared to listen to wise advice from people who have helped other boards improve.

How can a board improve itself? The best way is to invite an outside expert to evaluate its functionality. A board that is serious about constant improvement will be prepared to listen to wise advice from people who have helped other boards improve.

Additionally, a number of best practices for boards will include some of the following:

- Complete a formal certification for the organization and the board that requires having specific policies and processes in place. Most of these processes are outlined by the certifying agency. A number of certifying organizations exist in North America. The value in the exercise of becoming certified is that it ensures that the board and the organization document key practices and ensure that the practices are followed.

- Require all incoming board members to have, or obtain, professional board governance credentials from a recognized university or institute of advanced learning. Several high-profile universities now offer courses on governance, and board members should avail themselves of this kind of training.

- Develop a set of guiding principles for the exercise of board governance. This includes having clear expectations around the things that will, and will not, be part of the agenda of a board meeting. It may also include guidelines that govern board meeting participation and outline expectations of board members beyond the basics of a typical board manual.

- Establish specific expectations as part of the ongoing recruitment process for board members and include them in the new board member orientation package. These should go as far as outlining some expected communication behaviours. An orientation package may even specify things that board members should avoid doing (like providing task guidance to employees or speaking to the press on behalf of the organization unless authorized to do so). Wherever clarity is missing, people tend to invent their own guidelines or they import their expectations from previous experiences.

- Set out specific term limits for board members, and provide an orderly rotation of service and a framework that promotes a retention of corporate memory. Quite a few boards prescribe term limits of between two and four years, with one potential renewal (at the discretion of the board). This ensures that any board member who fails to contribute effectively is unlikely to remain on the board for an extended period, but it provides for the possibility that exceptional board members can agree to have their term renewed. In the end, board members should not serve beyond a continuous period of six to eight years, other than in exceptional situations. Some boards establish a role called a "continuity board member" to respond to the concern that corporate memory can evaporate. This role may be filled by a well-respected board member who has completed their term but is invited to continue to attend meetings for a set period of time as a non-voting member and is given the important task of being capable of providing context for decisions that were made in the past.

- Commit to ensuring that each board meeting contains some governance-related training or a brief review of specific board principles. Some boards read a brief "mantra" at the beginning of every meeting that underlines what they will focus on. This serves as a reminder of the scope of the meeting, and it can also set out principles for respectful dialogue. If a board meeting strays from the agreed framework, any board member can use the "mantra" to re-focus the conversation. A high functioning board can monitor its own behaviour. A board that never talks about how it ought to operate will eventually default to procedures and routines that could inadvertently include some bad habits.

> A board that never talks about how it ought to operate will eventually default to procedures and routines that could inadvertently include some bad habits.

CHAPTER 8
Can community organizations become the disruptors rather than the disrupted?

You don't drown by falling in the water; you drown by staying there.
—Edwin Louis Cole

In a chronically leaking boat, energy devoted to changing vessels is more productive than energy devoted to patching leaks.
—Warren Buffett

THE PROBLEM: CBNPs must change before a major crisis forces them to do so.

There is an immediate need to change the way that complex social problems are addressed. Charity and the old understanding of the charitable approach must be replaced by problem-solving efforts grounded in measurement and an outcome orientation. For the past 100 years, CBNPs have tried to use the principles of charity to do things that charity alone cannot do. The public has consistently ignored the failures of charitable efforts by celebrating its isolated successes. Generous donors to noble causes have been conditioned to respond emotionally and spontaneously, rather than logically and strategically. Funding agencies like foundations and governments are addicted to "social patches" and have established less than optimal criteria for funding projects and initiatives.

The problems that CBNPs seek to eliminate—the existence of discrimination, ongoing social isolation, systemic poverty, chronic homelessness or hunger, and the abuse of the vulnerable—cannot be solved by making a series of small adjustments. If lasting solutions are the objective, then everyone has to change what they are doing. Major change is often disorderly and unsettling.

> If lasting solutions are the objective, then everyone has to change what they are doing. Major change is often disorderly and unsettling.

If CBNPs continue to do the things they have done in the 20th century, then the problems of the 21st century will not diminish. Organizations that are invested in efforts to introduce change and reconciliation will not be able to advocate for those who are marginalized with any degree of credibility if they resist changing their strategies and tactics. Everyone claims to be doing good work even though a lot of emergency work in the social sector is little more than good-hearted patch work. CBNPs are furiously applying patches to problems that should not exist. Of course, temporary patches are sometimes essential. The problem is that if CBNPs only concentrate on patch work, the problems will expand. In 21st-century business language, the CBNP segment is ripe for disruption.

How will it be disrupted? The answer isn't a simple one. Will it come from radical changes in donor behaviour? Will it come from a complete overhaul of government policy? Will it come from within the sector? Will a new delivery model or new organization emerge in the sector the way that business disruptors have altered the commercial landscape in many industries? Will the aftermath of the COVID-19 pandemic completely change the way that CBNPs are funded? (For an opinion on that, see Appendix 4 at the end of this book).

The opportunity for disruption may depend on the specific challenges each sub-sector of the CBNP sector faces. For example, the realities of organizations that address LGBTQ2S concerns are very different from those that address the challenges of food security or child welfare. The answers will also be influenced by local community realities. Population size, density, and demographics will play a role. Some issues cross over a variety of sub-sectors. For example, many North American communities face major challenges in addressing the legitimate needs of its marginalized indigenous populations. This is not just a social issue but also a broader nation-to-nation issue that is far from one-dimensional. It will require extensive consultation with the stakeholders and enormous government investments.

The problem of chronic homelessness, which affects different demographic sub-populations, is a perfect example where one size does not fit all. There are a number of specific realities that vary by geography and by people group. Infrastructure factors also come into play. In Los Angeles County, over 40,000 people experience homelessness every day, and the majority are unsheltered. According to the coalition for the homeless, there were more than 62,000 people who were homeless in the New York City area in 2018. Both places have been dealing with a crisis, but the approach to the crisis is different due to factors like climate, availability of housing stock, political alignment, and differences in approach to coordinated housing access in each location. At the same time, a number of cities in North America have been able to achieve significant progress in the reduction of chronic homelessness. Whenever such progress is observed, common factors include the rigorous use of measurement, alignment of policy by different levels of government, long-term funding commitments, and carefully coordinated initiatives by local CBNPs with institutional capacity.

In this chapter, we will summarize some of the new ways of thinking that CBNPs need to apply to progress from the status quo towards a future that is outcome-oriented rather than activity driven.

A Story About an Unusual Pilot

> It was well below zero Fahrenheit in early January 2006, when I prepared to board a Continental Airlines flight at Montreal's Trudeau airport that was destined for Cleveland, Ohio. The flight was scheduled to leave at 6:05 a.m. That meant that I had to arrive at the airport before 4:45 a.m. so that I could go through the airline traveller's international check-in routine.
>
> First, there is the line-up to complete a self-check-in with the airline. This is followed by a series of verifications, including security screening and the formal Customs and Immigration interview—a very brief conversation with a US Customs officer. She or he confirms your travel plans focusing on your return date. Passport stamped, you are now free to walk to the gate.
>
> When everything runs smoothly, this set of processes takes about 30 minutes. On bad days, it can exceed an hour. On this particular day, the staff began the boarding process precisely at 5:40, and I grabbed my computer bag and my coffee and ambled to my pre-selected seat, 3A. I began to think about the agenda of the strategic planning meeting that I was going to facilitate. My thoughts were interrupted by a warm and friendly voice booming out over the intercom. "Welcome to our airplane this morning. I am your captain."
>
> I braced myself for the usual irrelevant information that airline pilots love to announce. After all, do we really care that we are going to taxi out to runway twenty-four left? Do we need to know that the "ceiling" at our destination is around 8000 feet with visibility of two miles? This is information that matters to the pilot but is of little relevance to the average traveller. That is not what happened that morning!

> The upbeat, enthusiastic tone that the captain used was so compelling in his opening sentence that I grabbed a pen and began taking notes on the little napkin that I had been using to hold my coffee. Speaking very clearly, and with energy and passion, his next sentences went like this.
>
> *"Ladies and Gentlemen, we are really happy that you are here. We're in business to fly—that's what we do! We have received our papers from the airport officials so we are now LEGAL to fly. We have a flight plan up here in the cockpit to tell us how we're going to get to Cleveland this morning. We know WHERE to fly. You may have seen the truck parked just off the right-hand side of the aircraft; that truck was filling us up with fuel. The tanks have been filled, so it is POSSIBLE to fly. Here in the cockpit, we have coffee, and at this hour, coffee makes us WILLING to fly. We have Susan on board; she is the nice flight attendant who greeted you, and she makes it FUN for everybody to fly. Then we have you! We're going to close the cabin door because you are all on board this morning. You are the REASON why we fly. So, from the cockpit, we invite you to sit back and relax...and LET'S...GO...FLYING!!!!!!!!!"*
>
> Everyone on the plane looked each other. Smiles were exchanged. People commented. Someone expressed the hope that the pilot's flying skills were as good as his announcements. I do not remember anything further about that flight—other than that the aircraft arrived in Cleveland at the scheduled time. The pilot, whose name I did not hear, will stay in my mind for a long time. Why? Because he used humour to outline many of the vital components that are needed in large and small organizations, for profit or non-profit.
>
> The pilot's announcement did not contain revolutionary insights or new concepts, but even if it had been delivered in a muffled monotone, it would still have been interesting. The fact that it was delivered with tremendous enthusiasm simply made us pay attention.

It is possible to dissect and analyze this cockpit announcement in at least a dozen ways. It was an unusual experience that makes an interesting story. More importantly, the pilot outlined an approach that any enterprise, including any CBNP, should consider if they want to make significant or revolutionary changes in the way that they approach what they do. In other words, there is a recipe for disrupting the status quo if the people in the CBNP sector want to do the disrupting themselves, rather than waiting for circumstances to do it for them.

> There is a recipe for disrupting the status quo if the people in the CBNP sector want to do the disrupting themselves, rather than waiting for circumstances to do it for them.

The pilot began by identifying the **CAUSE** or the purpose for his organization: "We're in business to fly—that's what we do." He also narrowed down the specifics. The plane was not just going to fly. It was going to fly on a specified route to a specified destination. Then he mentioned the need for a set of documents that clear the plane to fly to an international destination. In an organization, this kind of documentation is synonymous with well-established and understood **PROCESSES**. Every organization has critical processes and steps that need to be followed in order to serve clients. It would be unthinkable to take off and then discover that the plane was not permitted to land at its intended destination. The next thing the pilot mentioned was fuel. Every organization needs **RESOURCES**. The tank, large or small, has to be filled up with the fuel of resources in order to be able to get somewhere.

Next, he commented on his own **WILLINGNESS** to fly the plane. It was a bit of joke, but we've all observed people who show up every day in our organizations and perform in ways that make it very obvious that they are not particularly willing to their jobs. Great strategies go nowhere without engaged teams of people. These people make it **FUN** for each other to execute on the strategy on a day-to-day basis. The pilot's acknowledgement of the flight attendant highlighted the camaraderie of their team. The way he said it made it clear that Susan was an equally important team member. The captain of the aircraft has responsibilities, but so does the flight attendant.

Finally, the pilot delivered the punch line. Essentially, an organization could have all of the things that the pilot had previously mentioned, but they had to bear in mind that they were in business to serve **CLIENTS**. If there were no real clients, with real needs and expectations, then the activities would be meaningless. The passengers on the aircraft were the reason why all of the rest of the elements had to come together.

The lessons from this pilot's greeting are perfectly applicable in the world of CBNPs. When an organization can put all of these pieces together, they will position themselves to be change agents, radically altering the way things are done. Change agents are needed in a sector that is ripe for disruption. Given the compelling needs that CBNPs are addressing, they must either disrupt the status quo or they will be unceremoniously disrupted.

Establish Cause Clarity

Every CBNP has to establish cause clarity. That sounds simple, but it is far from easy to do. A passenger airline exists to transport passengers. Many organizations experience something called "mission drift." This is, as the label suggests, a gradual thing. It can happen over a period of years as peripheral activities or initiatives take centre stage and the core purpose becomes fuzzy. Disruption will be a threat to a CBNP that is drifting. Non-profits typically start up because someone sees a problem and is determined to do something about it. Frequently, they discover that the clients that they serve have additional needs, so they add programs or services.

> Many organizations experience "mission drift."

An organization that tries to do too many things with limited resources can become very busy and moderately ineffective at the same time. The question is: Can the organization's primary purpose be summarized coherently in a sentence or two? Do all of the employees and volunteers know what it is? One of the most important things that the organization's leaders can do is to frame the purpose and repeat it over and over again. Leaders should repeat the reason why the organization exists, ad nauseam!

Another important discipline is to evaluate activities, programs, or processes by determining the extent to which they are aligned with the primary cause. If a CBNP's primary cause is to provide access to sports programs for disadvantaged families then should the organization also be trying to provide food baskets? Should it be collecting and distributing clothing? Should it be cooking and distributing meals for seniors? The answer could be either yes or no depending on the realities in a particular community. The question does need to be asked.

Follow clear processes

Every CBNP needs to ensure that sound processes are in place to deliver the desired outcomes. Not only do proper processes have to be in place, they need to be visible. In other words, they should be observable to anyone who interacts with the CBNP. This may require some additional things like clear expectations around how client interactions happen, the oversight of evidence-based procedures, maintaining appropriate documentation, and conducting consistent evaluations. Organizations that operate based on the whims of team members or volunteers are ripe for disruption. If organizations seek to address social challenges in their communities, they cannot be haphazard or sloppy. Everyone wants to fly on airplanes that have pilots and airline management who place an enormous amount of importance on following sound processes that are constantly being updated, based on fresh data. Similarly, effective processes are vital in the non-profit world. Most CBNPs get started on a shoestring, and they fail to formally establish and then update their processes.

> Organizations that seek to address social challenges in their communities cannot be haphazard or sloppy.

Ensure that resources are obtained

Every CBNP needs to obtain and marshal resources to get the job done. An aircraft with no fuel cannot take off. A CBNP that has no money will struggle to fulfill its mission and mandate. Many small non-profits expect to obtain funding from governments and foundations, but they do not place any importance on the routine disciplines of searching for the resources they require. The cause rarely funds itself. Sitting back and expecting resources to flow in because the "need is great" usually results in disappointment and frustration.

> The cause rarely funds itself.

At the same time, CBNPs ought to jettison a "scarcity mentality" where every funding decision is viewed through the lens of a zero-sum game where every CBNP is seen to be in competition for donors with other CBNPs. An emerging paradigm is one where organizations are finding creative ways to partner together and raise awareness that identifies solutions to a social concern. This results in elevating awareness of the cause. The outcome is that everyone gains because more resources flow to the overall cause. In marketing terms, this is called "growing the market" rather than merely trying to steal market share from a competitor.

Recruit and develop motivated people

Every CBNP needs to recruit and develop people who are willing and capable. As important, the people who are face to face with disadvantaged clients need to be empathetic. Sometimes people join non-profit organizations because they have capabilities that are helpful to the organization, but they eventually end up treating their role as a weekly paycheque, rather than as a calling to participate in something vitally important. When chronic complaints arise among employees that centre entirely on their own wants and needs, then the dominant culture on the front lines can be about "me." Any organization that ignores its employees is usually headed in the wrong direction. If, on the other hand, the preferences of employees become the driving force for every decision, then the needs of the clients or beneficiaries will take second place.

> Organizations that serve the needs of the vulnerable must employ people who are committed to excellence and are prepared to go the extra mile.

Fun and laughter

Every CBNP needs to create an atmosphere of joy in the routines of day-to-day work. Dealing with people in difficulty can exhaust those who are intervening. Hearing heart-breaking stories can be emotionally draining. Representing people who experience senseless injustice can produce cynicism. That's why joy is important. It is why hope is important. Those who seek to accompany people who are vulnerable, exploited, or hurting need to develop genuine hope and exude it. Joy, hope, and fun are an antidote for the challenges that inevitably overtake those who seek to address the more unpleasant realities in our communities.

> Joy, hope, and fun are an antidote for the challenges that inevitably overtake those who seek to address the more unpleasant realities in our communities.

Client focus

It is interesting that some CBNPs that claim to exist to serve clients have institutionalized practices that are not remotely client-centric. These organizations are very likely to experience disruption. As an example, some CBNPs post pieces of paper all over their building to outline their rules. Most of them are phrased negatively. "Don't throw towels in the corner," or "You can only sit in this spot for five minutes." One important step that every CBNP should consider is to stop posting "rules" (except for safety signs). Safety guidelines should be on official signs, not on pieces of paper taped to walls. Arbitrary rules of behaviour need to be replaced by expectations. An expectation is an understanding that is established between the organization and the client. An organization may require respectful behaviour, but it is seldom a good idea to tape pieces of paper to the wall that tell clients in BIG BOLD LETTERS that they have to show respect to the staff. Sometimes organizations need outside help to identify annoying rules or bureaucratic procedures that can make access to their programs or services challenging. If the organization purports to serve those in need, it has to make sure that it isn't merely making things easy for its staff and volunteers and treating its clients as if they are lucky to be given any attention or that they'll only get assistance if they behave.

In addition to paying close attention to the principles articulated by the Continental pilot, there are four ways that CBNPs can "disrupt themselves" and avoid being compelled to make changes due to external pressures.

1. Develop An Outcome Orientation

CBNPs need to have an outcome orientation with defined milestones that lead towards measurable results.

Identifying milestones may be easy for a pilot flying a commercial aircraft. The pilot's ultimate goal is to park the airplane at the gate in the destination city. Along the way, there are specific milestones that include take-off, achieving cruising altitude, commencing descent, and landing, to name a few. Some will suggest that this is not easy in a CBNP. It is certainly more fluid. Working to address social challenges is never a purely linear and time-bound exercise. Progress on major changes in societal understanding and treatment of issues like discrimination, addiction, or violence has never happened quickly, or without institutional resistance. In many cases, it has been necessary to influence public opinion via education before a change could be proposed. Sometimes milestones can be achieved, and then progress might slow or even be reversed. This can be very frustrating and can demotivate the most ardent activist.

The imperative to make changes in how CBNPs function should never detract from the efforts of people who, with the best of intentions, have devoted their lives to the service of others. Everyone should have a deep appreciation for those who unselfishly invest their lives serving those who subsist in the shadows or who have been victimized by predators. People who serve the disadvantaged and refuse to ignore suffering, discrimination, and social injustice should be honoured. Their passion and their dedication must be celebrated. However, when someone has dedicated a good part of their life to the cause, they can sometimes develop a bit of myopia that is linked to excessive proximity to the issues. The challenge of being immersed in the daily realities of those who are marginalized is that there is a tendency to be overcome by the profound reality of human brokenness. This can make it difficult to step back and realistically assess what a path forward ought to look like. To re-use the overused metaphor, there is a tendency for CBNP workers to be very good at seeing the individual trees, while being unable to take stock of the forest.

> People who serve the disadvantaged and refuse to ignore suffering, discrimination, and social injustice should be honoured.

It is important to underline that the solutions being proposed will not be suitable for every single organization. The sheer number of different challenges is too broad and complex. Proposing solutions to help CBNPs deliver sustainable results is not an easy task. However, **the formula is not enormously different from the approach the pilot took in the story**. There is an assumption that the normal rules for success simply do not apply in the non-profit world. This assumption must be debunked. Yes, there are considerable differences between how most for-profit organizations function when compared with the operations of a CBNP. But there are also many similarities. One of the similarities is that every organization must constantly re-examine its assumptions and re-evaluate its value proposition. Far too many CBNPs operate from an untested set of assumptions. Far too many also struggle to articulate their real purpose. They can talk about what they do, but they may not be able to succinctly outline what they aim to achieve, or how their services are catalyzing measurable change. They can speak in emotional terms about the problems in the community, and they can provide a long list of noble activities they are undertaking, but all too often, they are not capable of explaining how what they are doing is crucial and imperative to the change they want to see. Furthermore, there is often a great deal of resistance to any third-party attempt to evaluate the impact of the activities they pursue.

2. Move from Mere Advocacy to Realistic Proposals

CBNPs need to develop the discipline of proposing ideas that are pragmatic and possible.

> Some CBNPs make a lot of noise, but not a lot of sense.

Some CBNPs that see themselves as advocates for change can become identified as chronic complainers. They make a lot of noise, but not a lot of sense. Some will march, protest, hold assemblies, and invite those who hold similar views to express outrage. They feel affirmed if they gain some traction in the media, but they are frequently unable to help shift public opinion. The news media might like to run a story or two because they typically love a controversial quote, and they will provide a platform from time to time to individuals who can provide them with colourful stories. Unfortunately, those who major in complaining seldom propose workable solutions. These CBNPs are likely to be disrupted by workable solutions that emerge from outside their sphere of influence.

A workable solution is anchored in reality and is consensus-driven. "Consensus-driven" does not mean that everyone agrees. It means that the actions proposed can be engineered or timed to generate broad support. Community groups are best advised to anchor their ideas in common sense. When CBNPs advocate strongly for unworkable proposals, they diminish their own credibility and find themselves sidelined. Many community-based social service organizations are better at identifying what is wrong than they are at developing practical, easy-to-implement ways to resolve the problems and make it right.

Those who define themselves as "community activists" tend to limit their prescribed solutions to a familiar cocktail of remedies. This can include a plethora of rather unrealistic demands for increased government funding. Community groups will seek out media coverage from time to time by claiming to need more money to avoid having to reduce or close a program. They will make a dramatic case that includes dire consequences should the funding not be forthcoming. The problem is that funds are finite, and governments can't do everything at the same time. Governments obtain the money they allocate to social services via taxation, and they proceed to redistribute it. The money does not magically appear out of thin air. It comes from taxpayers and is a consequence of wealth creation. If the economy isn't moving ahead, the amount of wealth that will be available for redistribution will be limited. Furthermore, simply providing more money to fund random responses to social challenges is not the best way to resolve them.

> Many community-based social service organizations are better at identifying what is wrong, than they are at developing practical, easy-to-implement ways to resolve the problems and make it right.

Ross Perot once famously said: "If you see a snake, just kill it—don't appoint a committee on snakes." The non-profit community loves committee meetings and is addicted to consultative processes. Some colleagues in the non-profit sector spend an inordinate amount of time in lengthy round table consultations with other organizations and the preparation of position papers and manifestos. Others are adept at organizing demonstrations, sending out online petitions, and requesting meetings with government officials. Social media has served to multiply the channels that can be used to gain attention. The problem is that social media posts typically produce very little in the way of measurable outcomes. They often succeed in making the person who posted the item feel validated. A well-orchestrated march can generate a short amount of attention in the traditional media, but such coverage is usually quickly forgotten or lost in the news cycle. The public moves on rather quickly to a new story or a different tragedy. Social media exchanges can raise the noise level (and start arguments), but they seldom change anyone's perspective nor do they help an organization to help more people in need.

Many ideas that are promoted by community-based non-profit organizations are not grounded in fiscal responsibility because community workers or activists have had limited exposure to the fiscal disciplines of the private sector. There is an assumption that increased funding directed towards community organizations will automatically produce better outcomes. Throwing money at a problem is rarely the best answer. The other hard truth is that some funding is not used wisely due to systemic inefficiencies within the community of non-profit organizations.

> There is an assumption that increased funding directed towards community organizations will automatically produce better outcomes. Throwing money at a problem is rarely the best answer.

3. Eliminate Duplication Wherever Possible

CBNPs must be unafraid to eliminate redundancies.

It seem politically incorrect or "cold" to suggest that CBNPs need to become more efficient in the way that they manage themselves and deploy resources. This perspective is frequently dismissed as "heartless." After all, doesn't everyone agree that CBNPs are chronically under-resourced? Sure, most are. The more acute concern should be that it is "heartless" to serve the disadvantaged and the vulnerable in an inefficient manner. Inefficiencies mean that those in need will receive less than they deserve, and precious resources will not be maximized. When a CBNP operates sub-optimally, clients are not treated with dignity, fewer clients are served, and fewer needs are met.

> Private funders and government agencies should carefully develop strategic partnerships with fewer organizations and, in some cases, require CBNP organizations to partner with each other in order to consolidate efforts.

Private funders and government agencies should carefully develop strategic partnerships with fewer organizations and, in some cases, require CBNP organizations to partner with each other in order to consolidate efforts. It is downright laughable to have four tiny food banks that operate within a few city blocks of each other, while steadfastly refusing to collaborate or consolidate. It is not a good use of resources for government agencies to fund multiple umbrella groups so that they can duplicate their advocacy work related to poverty reduction or housing rights within the exact same geographic area. There is also a legacy of duplication due to the fact that some community organizations were founded because one person left an existing organization to found his or her own CBNP. This has often resulted in competing non-profit organizations with the same cause that claim to serve similar needs in the same community.

That does not mean that sector-wide disruption has to be merger-crazy and that smaller CBNPs will disappear. There are plenty of good reasons for small CBNPs to exist. Many serve very specific needs and have well-developed capabilities. However, it is not very difficult to find examples of duplication of services in the non-profit sector. Some will explain that these duplications have geographical explanations or serve slightly different sub-populations. Does the duplication of services truly serve to add value, or upon careful examination, can several organizations combine their efforts and generate efficiencies rather than competing for legitimacy at the expense of those they ought to be serving?

> Can several organizations combine their efforts, rather than competing for legitimacy at the expense of those they ought to be serving?

Some might make the case that a few CBNPs could be eliminated if the government stepped in and took control of the issues with which CBNPs are dealing. However, governments in North America have consistently proven that they cannot do what the non-profit sector can do. They certainly cannot do it cost effectively.

Governments can, and must, set out policy frameworks that can be operationalized by CBNPs. In turn, the non-profit sector has to be strongly incentivized to act in an aligned manner. Government funding cannot continue to be determined by broad concepts of "being fair" to every noisy non-profit that is able to draw attention to their worthy cause. Funders can target funding where there is evidence of impact. This may include disproportionately funding CBNPs that deliver essential services and are changing the equation in their area of service. They may be eliminating duplication by doing things like developing strong community-level partnerships, providing innovative wrap-around services that are carefully targeted, and ensuring a continuum of care whereby the needs of clients transcend the preferences of the CBNP.

4. Develop a Data-driven Approach to Secure Funding

CBNPs must collect, harness, and make effective use of real-time data.

Forward thinking CBNPs are already beginning to employ reliable data to drive better decision-making. This, in turn, leads to greater operational efficiency. Those who resist proactively employing data that carefully targets specific outcomes and measures the impact of funds invested are vulnerable to outside disruption. Increasingly, funding is linked to a set of outcomes rather than as a means to fuel a project or sustain a program. It is somewhat unpopular to talk about ROI (return on investment) in the non-profit world. However, funding agencies and private donors cannot continue to provide funds to organizations based solely upon a perception that they "do good work."

> Funding agencies and private donors cannot continue to provide funds to organizations based solely upon a perception that they "do good work."

CBNPs typically feel successful if they gain ongoing media attention, if a quasi-celebrity takes up the cause, or if they secure a meeting with a sympathetic government minister who promises to have their department officials study a proposal. Each is validating for the organization, but these are seldom helpful in the medium term. Media attention and celebrity endorsements may extend some temporary assistance to an organization, but they are difficult to sustain. Government priorities change, and the attention span of political parties is limited. The other challenge is that the issues that concern most CBNPs are not issues that help elect candidates. Political parties will always campaign on pocketbook issues or respond to the concerns and fears of the electorate. There is occasionally some flirtation with things like funding for senior care, increased family benefits, or tax breaks for the poor. However, they are typically designed to respond to the broadest possible group of potential voters. Virtually no political candidate runs on a platform that includes eliminating complex social issues because it isn't an issue for the majority of the people who will turn out at the polling station. Furthermore, very few politicians will stake out a position that favours providing major increases in funding for non-profit organizations.

The path forward, one that will engage everyone, includes using technology to produce reliable information and to anchor proposals firmly in facts. For the past 50 years, data and facts have been hard to nail down. This has been partly due to the inability to harmonize input of information and collect meaningful statistics. It has also been partly due to the unwillingness or inability of CBNPs to measure their effectiveness. Data, like how many individual people come to a drop-in centre, can be elusive, because workers or volunteers typically count visits per day. Therefore, if the daily count of people totalled 40 and the centre was open for 22 days of the month, the message that would go out is that "we served 880 people this month." However, what is often difficult to assess is whether this is 880 unique individuals or if the same 40 people dropped in every day, and if their presence at the drop-in centre resulted in any meaningful change in their status.

How can we get started?

A good place to start is to change the narrative when addressing the people in government who are responsible for framing policy. CBNPs should stop complaining about what the government is not doing and propose pragmatic solutions. A good approach is to ask politicians or senior level civil servants to share their views on what the future for the disadvantaged needs to look like. Far too often, the approach to meetings with government officials is one where a laundry list of complaints is articulated, along with an equally long list of funding requests. Government ministers and ministry departments compete internally for budgets. Every group they meet is asking for more money, forcing them to juggle a variety of competing priorities. CBNPs need to abandon a begging posture when interacting with government funders. The classic "FUND ME" approach is increasingly unproductive.

> CBNPs should stop complaining about what the government is not doing and propose pragmatic solutions.

Ultimately, CBNPs must develop a solution-orientation by learning to apply some principles that exist in forward-moving organizations in the for-profit world. Does this mean that CBNPs have to become just like corporations? Not at all. Simply put, there is merit in studying best practices outside the non-profit sector to discover practices that can be adapted in the non-profit sector.

At our Mission, we operate free grocery stores for people who live below the poverty line. Clients do not have to line up to get in to our Marché. They do not receive a box of canned food. Instead they have membership cards with their photo on the card and enjoy a grocery shopping experience that is somewhat similar to the experience anyone might have at a small market. Approximately 75% of the food that is available is perishable. This includes fresh fruits, vegetables, dairy products, and meat. The food is recuperated from grocery stores and producers in the area by one of our valued partners, an organization called Moisson Montreal. We operate a fleet of refrigerated trucks that allows us to pick up pallets full of fresh items at Moisson Montreal's warehouse and then bring it to our sorting center to triage products quickly and get them into the grocery stores. Clients arrive by appointment within a prescribed time block and they have the opportunity to select what they want. Quantities are limited based on the size of their family.

Some time ago, while taking a donor through one of our innovative free grocery stores, the donor turned to me and asked, "When you set up this system, did you copy all of the best practices of food banks?" I responded, "No, we ignored them, and we copied the best practices of grocery stores." We copied a for-profit approach because we believe that people experiencing food insecurity should not have to accept a handout. We believe that they should have a legitimate shopping experience. So when a volunteer at the checkout scans their products we are able to know what inventory items were selected (a business principle) and the client has a real shopping experience, with one exception. The groceries are free.

Will this approach resolve the challenge of food security? On its own, not at all. However, it does elevate the sense of dignity of those in need by allowing them to exercise agency. For our organization, food and shelter are mere entry points for those in need. Loving our clients is our "secret sauce." Our objectives include working with partners to end chronic homelessness and hunger in our part of the world. In our view this includes responding to needs by walking alongside the vulnerable on their pathway back towards independence. We like it when clients are able to say, "I don't need your services any longer."

> For our organization, food and shelter are mere entry points for those in need. Loving our clients is our "secret sauce."

CHAPTER 9
Where are the opportunities?

To succeed, jump as quickly at opportunities as you do at conclusions.
—Benjamin Franklin

*The activist is not the man who says the river is dirty;
the activist is the man who cleans up the river.*
—H. Ross Perot

Over the past century, the public has generally believed that pockets of poverty would exist. Expectations shifted somewhat in the last half of the 20th century. Still, most people continued to accept the premise that many of the people who fell between the cracks did so because they lacked initiative. It was socially acceptable to be just a little bit suspicious of anyone who tentatively reported that they had suffered physical, sexual or psychological abuse. Nobody understood the lasting impact of trauma and disconnection, particularly within indigenous communities who were stripped of their culture and forcibly separated from their families.

The theory that addictions were the result of a weakness of character or a function of personal choice was widely accepted. It was considered perfectly normal in polite society to toss mild racial slurs into a conversation or to make snide remarks about a person's sexual orientation. Practices that were broadly tolerated resulted in a pervasive culture of discrimination against women and allowed stereotypes to persist in our culture. Some phrases have endured in our lexicon. For example, "giving someone the bum's rush" is a direct reference to the way it was acceptable to treat someone who was considered a "lowlife" or a "drifter" at the turn of the 20th century.

In the face of the prevailing culture, the kind people who serve at community-based non-profit organizations have been tireless caregivers by providing help and care to the marginalized. These people stood up for the downtrodden, even when their own efforts were less than perfect. Their voices have advocated for change. The main problem in the third decade of the 21st century is that the need to change is confronting the people who have been busy helping the disadvantaged. Change has caught up with the advocates of social change.

Front-line workers in any CBNP will say that the number one barrier to change for their clients is their willingness to take the first, very difficult steps towards wanting to change. They will say that many people in precarious situations have to "find a reason to feel the need to change." The same is true for the leadership of the CBNP sector. Change is usually impossible if the organizational culture is one of "excusitis"—defined as the ability to find excuses that outline why change isn't possible. CBNPs are sometimes oblivious to the fact that they operate in a shifting environment. They may not envision a looming issue on the horizon that is forcing them to make dramatic changes. More often, most organizations simply walk from one mini-crisis to another, unable to take a step back and look at the bigger picture. This challenge is amplified if a CBNP suffers from stagnant leadership or less than enlightened governance.

The question that can be asked is: Will the players themselves be the catalysts for change, or will the sector have changes imposed on it? This book has been deliberately constructed to describe in the broadest terms the challenges that many CBNPs face. It does not propose to have all the answers.

This runs deeper than making minor adjustments to the structure of CBNP organizations or their offer of service. Someone once said that a manifesto is a problem stated in reverse. Therefore, if the problem is defined as doing things that do not produce lasting or measurable outcomes, then the reverse of the challenge should be obvious. What would happen if CBNPs declared that they would invest energy to obtain relevant data that allows them to accurately define the problem they seek to address, deploy innovative services that are impact-oriented, and use credible metrics to evaluate the results? What if their goal was to ensure that, after a reasonable period, most the services they are currently providing will no longer be required? What would happen if CBNPs aimed to put themselves out of business?

> This is an invitation to CBNPs to move away from merely doing the right things and consider doing the right things in the right way.

Opportunity 1: CBNPs must help the public shift from a "needs" orientation to a "results" orientation

Organizations that exist to respond to community needs must help donors and partners change the way they respond to perceived social challenges. When confronted with a tragedy, people are often inclined to act without adequately assessing the problem or investigating what is already being done about it. Donors, if they want to become more helpful, need to stop making one-time donations to a need. They should seek to identify an outcome and partner over the long haul with organizations that aim to achieve the outcome.

Spontaneous donations or funding campaigns can be ill advised, as can indiscriminate or ill-planned acts of goodness, even when they are the product of pure motives. For example, organizations that respond to the needs of those experiencing homelessness are often contacted by people who feel compelled to put together small "care packages" and then go to a downtown park and hand them out to people they see who look like they may be in difficulty. On the surface, this may seem like a caring and thoughtful response. The problem is that very few people understand the daily struggles and the real needs of those who find themselves on the street. Giving a sandwich, a bar of soap and some other personal hygiene items does very little to respond to the challenge that the person in the park is facing. Someone who doesn't have a home needs housing, not a bar of soap or a cup of coffee. Groups of concerned people are better advised to transfer their energy (and any funds that they could raise) into providing ongoing support for a well-recognized organization that is actively responding to the needs of those experiencing homelessness.

Some people who encounter a particular social problem might be inclined to attempt to launch an effort to fix the situation themselves, without giving any thought to its complexity. When someone sees or hears about human suffering, there can be an overwhelming impulse to react personally. An individual may hear a report about children in a neighbourhood who do not have shoes. They might immediately and run out to a shoe store, buy a big quantity of shoes, and hold a giveaway event in their garage. Someone else may rush to set up a fundraising campaign to raise funds that will provide free shoes to those in need via a social media platform. That kind of action assumes that an ad hoc effort is the best response. Most of the time, these responses end up being utterly inadequate. They are not sustainable and they address a symptom without acknowledging that the problem runs deeper than a pair of shoes. It is better to consolidate efforts by channelling energy and funding towards organizations that have the experience and infrastructure to obtain long term results. In other words, efforts need to be made to change the reality of the people in the neighbourhood rather than simply supply some shoes.

What would happen if CBNPs aimed to put themselves out of business?

If faced with traffic gridlock and vehicular congestion in a city, nobody would propose that individual citizens take matters into their own hands by getting out of their cars and walking into the middle of the road at all the major intersections with the goal of fixing the problem. Most people would agree that this would be both unwise and unsafe. Uncoordinated efforts by ill-equipped people is not a short or long-term solution to the problem. Very few people are equipped to understand the complexities of traffic patterns. Even fewer are experts in traffic management. Similarly, people who are overcome with compassion when faced with a complex social issue are not automatically infused with the expertise needed to resolve that issue. When it comes to responding effectively to issues that pull at our heartstrings, it is often better to support an organization that is already at work on the problem.

> People who are overcome with compassion when faced with a complex social issue are not automatically infused with the expertise needed to resolve that issue.

It is refreshing to observe concern or outrage on the part of members of the public when they become aware of a solvable problem. Informed people recognize that there isn't any reason why women should be subjected to violence. No woman ought to be living in fear of an abusive partner or former partner. It makes no sense that children go to bed hungry. Most people recoil in horror when they observe the precariousness of many indigenous people who find themselves subjected to drug dealers and other predators in our urban settings. Many have been tragically disconnected from their communities and their culture as a result of colonization. It is appropriate for all of us to want to do something to respond when we become aware of the plight of people who are suffering. However, our response to the righteous indignation that we feel has to be a thoughtful one. Potential donors must be encouraged to be well informed. Major social challenges cannot be resolved unless the actions taken are well coordinated. Citizens who are outraged by specific social issues can make a long-term commitment to align themselves with well-established organizations that are working on the front lines and can support them with money, time, and encouragement.

> Our response to the righteous indignation that we feel has to be a thoughtful one. Potential donors must be encouraged to be well informed.

There is another change that donors need to consider. The end-of-year bubble of donor activity is a bad habit that needs to change. To some extent, the non-profit sector has been responsible for creating it. Most CBNPs raise the largest part of their donations in October, November, and December. Everyone experiences the phenomenon of increased volunteerism at that time. Companies contact CBNPs offering to bring teams to prepare food, visit the lonely, sort clothing, or serve meals. Well-intentioned people line up to volunteer to deliver boxes of food at Thanksgiving and Christmas, as if hunger was only a problem in the fourth quarter of the year. Large quantities of warm clothing are donated even though winter clothing is best donated before winter begins because it can take weeks for organizations to sort the clothing and make it available. The challenges of poverty, exclusion, homelessness, abuse, and hunger don't diminish as a result of a concerted year-end blitz.

In January, February, and March, the same number of people still require assistance. Yet many donors feel like they have done their duty, even though their perception of duty may be a mere throwaway at the end of the calendar year.

Donors can become more sensitive to the reality that the challenges being addressed by CBNPs are rarely seasonal. The needs are a year-round reality; not something that happens at the end of the calendar year. People who are truly serious about solving social problems in their communities can develop the discipline of supporting outcomes rather than reacting to needs and providing financial resources.

> Donors can become more sensitive to the reality that the challenges being addressed by CBNPs are rarely seasonal.

Opportunity 2: CBNPs must be encouraged to forge partnerships and mergers to achieve better outcomes

Any reasonably objective assessment of the realities of the CBNP landscape will conclude that there are enormous opportunities for improved effectiveness within the sector if many of the fiercely independent organizations would consider joining forces. There are a variety of ways to join forces, but the ultimate goal has to include ensuring that they are better positioned to meet the needs of those who stand to benefit from their services. It is virtually impossible in our interconnected world for any organization to act independently and achieve optimal outcomes. Strategic partnerships, mergers and corridors of referral can help community-based non-profit organizations gain traction via increased capacity. Working together contributes to the achievement of better outcomes. A single organization can rarely provide a full continuum of care for all of its clients. Furthermore, two or three well-resourced CBNPs that work in close coordination usually have a bigger impact than a dozen chronically under-resourced organizations that work in isolation.

> Strategic partnerships, mergers and corridors of referral can help community-based non-profit organizations gain traction

via increased capacity. Working together contributes to the achievement of better outcomes.

The tendency for CBNPs to be detached—to operate alone—has led to a reality in which scarce resources are frequently misapplied. This can occur in the deployment of people and capital, but the most evident waste of energy happens in routine activities when an organization's efforts are focused on time-intensive activities that add little discernable value and produce no measurable outcomes. This misapplied energy is often the root cause of burnout, and it reduces the discernable effectiveness of the organization. Many community organizations promote their activities merely because they have secured some ongoing funding linked to a particular program.

CBNPs tend to resist mergers. The idea of merging or joining forces formally with another organization is usually a non-starter unless a CBNP faces a severe crisis. This seems to be rooted in a series of beliefs. Most community groups are firmly convinced that they are unique. Why should a CBNP consider merging? The direct answer is: **to serve clients better.**

Why do so few non-profits make serious attempts to evaluate their efficiencies and assess their operations from the perspective of their clients? Part of the reason is that many CBNPs have been conditioned to accept less than ideal outcomes. If the operation functions sub-optimally or lacks adequate capacity, the needs of its clients cannot be well served. If the organization resists change, unproductive activities will multiply. This can have an exponential negative effect within the ecosystem that the organization purports to serve.

It is very important to underline that this is NOT a clarion call for small organizations to be acquired by larger organizations. Many small organizations are very efficient and operate in a well-defined niche. This is not about being big or small, it is about becoming more effective and innovative. It is about finding new ways to meet evolving and emerging client needs rather than being anchored in beliefs and practices that resist any scrutiny.

This is not about being big or small, it is about becoming more effective and innovative.

The opportunity to develop real partnerships or facilitate mergers is an area where charities that function as financial consolidators have a role to play. Historically, organizations that have a mandate to collect money and redistribute it have acted as the principal fundraising partner for a number of smaller CBNPs. Some organizations have become dependent on the funding they obtain from agencies like Centraide or the United Way. Donors who give to consolidators expect that their donation will be broadly distributed according to priorities established by the leadership of the consolidator. In other words, when a donor gives $100 to United Way, an internal process at the United Way evaluates the requirements of its client agencies and divides the money using a variety of metrics. Organizations like the United Way need to continue to use their influence to push for efficiencies by encouraging merger discussions that will roll up similar CBNPs into a single, more efficient, entity. They can also encourage virtual partnerships within communities so that a client can move seamlessly from one CBNP to another and experience a continuum of care.

Opportunity 3: CBNPs must reframe how their effectiveness is evaluated

The complexity of non-profits has changed a great deal, but the way that their effectiveness is evaluated has not. Many individual donors tend to make their donation decisions based on a combination of perceptions and emotions. A donation that is driven entirely by emotion can be misguided. The same is true of a financial investment, like the purchase of a house. Still, donors will always make an emotional connection to an issue, and this can be the trigger for a donation. The larger issue has to do with the analytical errors that routinely occur when donors apply a less than ideal framework of financial analysis to the way they assess CBNPs.

In recent years, several charity-rating services have cropped up. They claim to be able to help potential donors assess the **efficiency** of their donated dollars. The problem is that these rating services seldom invest time visiting the organizations that they purport to evaluate. They simply establish a set of standard financial metrics or ratios, they gather publically available information from the internet, and then assess each specific organization using a grid that they create. This can lead to a variety of misunderstandings because one size does not fit all. There are significant differences in the funding realities and government oversight from state-to-state and province-to-province. The operational requirements of CBNPs do not always fit into neat boxes.

The other challenge is that, just like any other competitive ratings system, it is possible for CBNPs to work hard to deliberately achieve a high rating in order to look good in the ratings report. This means that they may be very efficient, or they may just have developed the ability to do things that are designed to generate good scores in the charity ratings game.

The biggest challenge is not rating agencies. It is an old, but well-accepted rule that persists in the non-profit world. Some refer to it as the overhead ratio. Funders and donors need to resist evaluating the efficiency of CBNP organizations based on ratios of administrative or fundraising dollars spent versus dollars spent on program delivery. Running effective programs requires management talent, qualified professional staff, and marketing and fundraising expenses. Some organizations can achieve outcomes with very little overhead. A street outreach operation may not need more than a small office space and a couple of computers. An organization that operates a sophisticated food distribution center or a series of sizeable housing facilities may need to invest in infrastructure that is costly to acquire, maintain and staff.

> Funders and donors need to resist evaluating the efficiency of CBNP organizations based on ratios of administrative or fundraising dollars spent versus dollars spent on program delivery.

It begins with a double standard that exists. Nobody is particularly concerned when a business spends money on marketing and sales, yet there is unease when a non-profit invests money to hire professionals who make it possible for the CBNP to generate awareness around the cause or conduct activities that raise money for it. Donors have traditionally tended to feel more comfortable if a CBNP is located in a sub-standard building that badly requires renovation and is run by people who live below the poverty line. However, if a CBNP is going to be effective it needs to pay staff salaries that are competitive, but reasonable. It ought to be considered unacceptable for an organization to pay people at rates that are barely above the minimum wage and expect them to respond to the needs of those living on the margins. The challenge is that the mindset of scarcity prevails. Most CBNPs will protest that they can't afford to pay more.

A different kind of thinking is needed. When discussions around expenses and compensation at CBNPs is raised concerns about excesses are often raised. We very seldom hear people say that it is scandalous that the workers in community-based non-profit organizations are so poorly paid. There have been a few isolated cases of misuse of funds by CBNPs and stories in the media about non-profit executives who are reported to have salaries and benefits that eclipse the remuneration packages of some corporate executives. These stories alarm donors but they are not the norm in the sector. Some CBNPs can operate by deploying volunteers but many need to hire well-qualified staff and management professionals who have the ability and experience to serve those in need. CBNPs need to compete for talent—social workers, medical professionals, leaders, and managers are in short supply.

There are persistent myths that exist around the cost of raising money for non-profits. Members of the public would be surprised to learn that there is a disproportionate cost associated with the acquisition of a new donor, but it is essential for organizations to invest money to ensure that are able to acquire new donors. In some cases, it costs up to $1.50 to obtain an initial $1.00 donation from a new donor. The acquisition cost is usually recovered when a first-time donor makes subsequent donations. Even organizations that obtain the majority of their funding via government programs or grants from foundations need to invest heavily in people and processes to send in applications, fill out funding requests, and produce volumes of reports. Unless governments alter the equation in the future, CBNPs will need to spend money to obtain funding. Funding does not just drift in. The question is: How much should a CBNP invest in fundraising? Is there a ratio? Most people would agree that an organization should not spend 80% of its revenues on fundraising efforts. Traditional wisdom says it should be as low as possible. Nonetheless, it is unclear what a "magic ratio" ought to be or how it ought to be measured.

> Community-based non-profit organizations need to spend money to obtain funding. Funding does not just drift in.

Donors have become accustomed to perceiving that a community organization is efficient if its overhead to program ratio is between 15-35%. This is not a good way of assessing a CBNP's administrative and fundraising operations. It is impossible to isolate the activity of helping from the essentials of administrative oversight. Furthermore, nothing happens without activities that generate resources or money. In most CBNPs, everyone should be involved in some aspect of promotion, communication, or stakeholder engagement. If stakeholders or potential donors are trying to assess an organization based on fundraising/program ratios, the following hypothetical scenario may provide some clarity.

> Let's suppose that, as a donor, you are considering making a $500 donation to one of two wonderful organizations. **Let's also assume that both organizations are reputable, hardworking, and actively addressing a cause that you support.** Last year, one of the organizations was able to raise $400,000 and spent $60,000 (15%) on fundraising and administration. The other organization was able to raise $4,000,000 and spent $1,000,000 (25%) on fundraising and administration. The first organization has $340,000 to operate, whereas the second one has $3,000,000. Which of the two can have a larger impact? The first organization will likely cover the rent, pay a couple of staff members, and run a program or two. Their people and programs might be under-resourced, but their spending to program funding ratio looks impressive.

> But did they really only spend $60,000? It impossible to know how many hours the client-facing staff quietly invested in fundraising at the expense of delivering services to those in need. The second organization will have quite a few strategic options available because they were able to obtain far greater resources. In most contexts $3,000,000 of operating funds can fuel a number of programs that can, in turn, produce a measurable impact. A donation to the first organization might not significantly change their ability to gain traction. A donation to the second organization might further an effort that already has the critical mass to achieve outcomes that are comparatively more substantial.
>
> This illustration is **not** meant to suggest that a small non-profit is inefficient or ineffective. It is certainly not intended to dismiss the validity or impact of small, narrowly focused CBNPs because **bigger does not mean better.** The point is simply that using an arbitrary ratio to compare two organizations that are engaged in a similar cause should not be the compelling factor in a donor's decision. Assuming that, as donors, there is a commitment to the principles of problem solving (rather than just seeking to be charitable), an organization with a higher fundraising ratio might be a perfectly valid option.

Donors and funding agencies need to be encouraged to begin to envision their donation as a partnership that aims to support a solution rather than as a bit of cash that aims to sustain an activity. When a donor makes this critical shift, the emphasis will move away from concerns about immediate needs or arbitrary ratios. Instead, donors and CBNPs will evaluate effectiveness by assessing the degree to which a CBNP is achieving results related to well-established objectives.

> Donors and funding agencies need to be encouraged to begin to envision their donation as a partnership that aims to support a solution rather than as a bit of cash that aims to sustain an activity.

Opportunity 4: CBNPs should be encouraged to consider growing their revenue through creative social enterprise initiatives

Increasingly, charitable organizations are being encouraged to consider finding ways to fund their programs by generating income through ongoing entrepreneurial activities. In practical terms, this means capitalizing and managing a business venture inside the organization. It can include employing people and generating recurring income for the organization. In many cases, this includes job creation for people who have employment challenges and providing meaningful activity and/or income for those who may not be able to occupy a traditional job.

This sometimes stirs up controversy. It may be legitimate to question if running a social enterprise potentially interferes with the primary purpose of the non-profit. If the organization is trying to respond to unmet requirements of families with special needs children, should it invest a large percentage of its efforts running a used furniture store to raise funds for the cause? Does a food service business staffed by volunteer labour obtain an unfair competitive advantage in marketing its services? Is the goal of the CBNP to sell food or furniture, or is it to run programs for its beneficiaries? At the same time, if it can be argued that if the revenue-generating social enterprise is well managed and provides employment to people in social reinsertion programs, it may be a reasonable way to generate a portion of the operating funds needed by the non-profit.

It is vital to recognize the possible pitfalls of developing non-traditional streams of revenue. The challenge of financing a non-profit via a social enterprise platform is that the experience and training of people who are running a community-based non-profit frequently do not include business management skills. It takes much more than passion and a good heart to open a restaurant, run a small farm, develop a catering business, run a recycling center, or manage a shop that sells used clothing or furniture.

When fundamental business acumen is missing, these efforts usually fall short, and the endeavour can actually reduce the revenue stream of the CBNP. It is important that a framework of rigorous cost accounting be applied to assess the viability of the operation. For example, a coffee shop or store that produces $700 per day of net revenue may have $600 per day of measurable costs and a further $200 per day of soft costs. Without proper accounting controls, costs can be misallocated, which will falsify the results. Proponents of social enterprise tend to talk more about top-line revenue than they do about bottom-line profit. Even if a social enterprise initiative is profitable, its cost ratio can exceed that of a standard fundraising effort. Donors who balk at contributing to an organization that spends 30 cents to obtain a dollar of revenue via traditional fundraising might run the other way if they knew that most non-profit social enterprises spend 85 or 90 cents to obtain a dollar.

It is important to underline that, while social enterprises are not the only pathway to address a CBNP's funding dilemma, they are often very important to its operations. They can add value to an organization's service offering or they can serve as an employment reinsertion platform. They may be part of the process of generating awareness for the cause and objectives of the organization and can serve as a backdrop for media mentions and volunteer recruitment. Some organizations are able to operate social enterprises efficiently and fund major parts of their operation via initiatives like cafés and thrift stores. Others have developed revenue streams in labour-intensive services like car washes, farms, and catering operations.

What can an individual member of the public do?

Members of the public must begin to recalibrate perceptions about how community-based non-profit organizations ought to operate. For too long, everyone has expected those who served the people in precarious situations to operate precariously! It was considered normal that they would use substandard technology and operate out of facilities that were ready for demolition. Most people forgave CBNPs for being delightfully inept, because they frequently employed people who were otherwise seen as unemployable. It was expected that they would always be short of funds, so everybody put up with their slightly hokey fundraising schemes. The public seldom bothered to grasp the details of the problems that these organizations were seeking to address and seemed genuinely pleased that someone was keeping the problem more or less out of sight. Many people still assume that most CBNPs obtain the majority of their funding from government agencies.

The public's perceptions of the value of the work that is undertaken day after day by non-profit groups in our communities has been forged by a variety of historical understandings. These understandings are fashioned by the way people were raised and influenced by the voices they listen to. These influences include friends and family, connections on social media, and the stories they consume in the traditional media. Prevailing prejudices or perspectives around issues like discrimination, poverty, and addiction cause every individual to adopt attitudes that, in turn, drive behaviours.

What thoughts go through our minds when we encounter people who are vulnerable or those who have fallen on hard times? Do we feel any sympathy? Do we assume that they are people who are lazy and ought to get their act together? Do we see them as clever manipulators of the social system, or do we perceive them as victims of injustice? Or, do we wonder if they might be people who are a lot like us who have run into a temporary rough spot in life?

> Most of the problems that CBNPs are trying to address are solvable—within a generation.

One of the things that this book aims to provoke is the sense that that everyone may have to "hit the reset button" and re-examine all of our perceptions in order to make any serious progress towards tackling the large number of solvable social challenges. The selection of the word "solvable" here is very deliberate. Most of the problems that CBNPs are trying to address are solvable—within a generation. The prevailing North American economic system dictates that it is entirely likely that the Western world will always face the realities of people who experience poverty and disconnectedness. Exploitation and discrimination have not shown any signs of disappearing. Capitalism, even carefully managed capitalism, will have winners and losers. Modern social and family structures are such that relational breakdowns are increasingly common.

The good news is that many of these social problems can be can be greatly reduced with an approach that targets the causes rather than the symptoms – an approach that takes careful aim the root of the issue and is prepared to make courageous decisions that may only produce measurable results several years down the road.

A few concluding suggestions

- We must help North American society move towards reconciliation and inclusion of those who identify with indigenous communities. For too long, prejudices and misconceptions have been tolerated and generational trauma has produced undeniable evidence of social disconnection that disproportionately impacts these communities.

- Structural changes are needed to reduce the sense of meaninglessness that many minority communities feel and the resulting social challenges that arise from generational poverty, lack of access to education, excessive incarceration, and poor housing.

- We must become serious about aligning efforts to eliminate chronic homelessness.

- We need to end hunger, particularly hunger that impacts children. There is no reason why anyone in North America should be hungry when policy initiatives can greatly reduce the number of people who have to choose between paying the rent and buying food at the beginning of each month. Furthermore, mega-quantities of surplus food can be recuperated and an effective distribution system can be set up to ensure that it can be provided to all who need it.

- No child should go to school under-equipped and without breakfast or lunch. Academic support programs need to be part of a strategy of eliminating the cycle of poverty rather than a haphazard domain of charitable efforts.

- Violence and aggression directed towards women and members of the LGBTQ2S community must become as unacceptable as smoking in an airplane.

- Abandonment of senior citizens or consignment of people to underfunded institutional settings is completely preventable.

- There is no logical reason why young people who are cared for by the state up until the age of majority ought to be deprived of ongoing support when they "age out" of the system.

The list could go on…and on…and on, but this book must have an end!

To conclude, here is a list of four steps that any interested person can take if they want to respond to those in need in their community:

Step 1: Find a compelling cause that matters. Stop giving small amounts of time or money to dozens of random endeavours. Don't be a reactive donor. Be a proactive and informed donor. Identify an issue that you are passionate about, and identify how you can make a difference. It could be environmental awareness, youth employment, the fight against sex trafficking, or any one of dozens of other important causes. The cause you select can be intensely personal. People who have provided care to those who suffered with chronic diseases are often compelled to get involved in the fight against those diseases. By narrowing your focus, you will be able to channel your efforts in a way that allows you to have more impact.

> Don't be a reactive donor. Be a proactive and informed donor.

Step 2: Align yourself with people who understand the cause and elevate your own awareness. Don't duplicate existing work or start an effort that you are not equipped to manage. Find organizations that are actively doing something to address the cause you have identified. Get to know what they do and how they do it. Research the cause and the organizations, and visit them if you can. Ask questions about outcomes. Listen to the language they use. Your impressions of the work they do will help you evaluate how you can become involved.

Step 3: Engage with the cause—don't just donate. Every community organization loves to receive donations. Yes, you should donate! As important as donors are, CBNPs also need people who will be active, informed ambassadors for their cause. Be strategic with your time and money. If you donate, do so year-round.

> Help isn't really help if it fails the tests of effectiveness or appropriateness.

Step 4: Share the message with your friends and family. The misconceptions and myths that persist around the community-based non-profit sector continue to prevent well-meaning people from having a real impact. Help isn't really help if it fails the tests of effectiveness or appropriateness. It isn't usually helpful unless it promotes dignity and includes a path towards wholeness that is designed around the aspirations of the person who is receiving the assistance. Encourage those that you know to participate in helping CBNPs, and suggest that they do so in an informed way.

AFTERWORD

In 2010, former Vice-Presidential candidate Sarah Palin spoke to an audience of Tea Party supporters in Nashville, Tennessee. In a scathing critique of the Obama administration, she mockingly asked, "How's that hopey, changey stuff working out for ya?"

While Ms Palin was looking to collect a laugh and deliver a politically charged zinger to a room full of receptive people, it is doubtful that she was suggesting that hope should be abandoned or that change was unnecessary. She probably wasn't declaring her opposition to change; she was probably being critical of a political slogan that she found unappealing. After all, change is the only constant. It is a fundamental law of the universe. The interesting thing is that the pace of change continues to accelerate exponentially, and it tends to be resisted by those who feel most threatened. On the other hand, the acceleration of change expands the available options and opportunities for those who embrace it.

Peter Drucker may have been among the first to recognize the disruptive potential of technological change, coupled with the realignment of social and economic structures at a worldwide level in his book *The Age of Discontinuity*, which was first published in 1969. He would undoubtedly feel vindicated in his predictions if he could see how the 21st century is unfolding.

It should not be an earth shattering idea to propose that change is coming to the community-based non-profit sector. Of course, it is coming! This book suggests that several changes are long overdue. Change may need to happen to ensure the survival of some CBNPs, but that is not the main point. The main point is that CBNPs must re-assess their traditional ways of thinking. Rather than trying to do more of what they have been doing, they must aim to achieve better outcomes for the people they serve. If they are unwilling to proactively disrupt themselves, they will be subject to externally driven disruption.

> In the face of change and destabilizing influences, it is even more critical that CBNPs be the agents of hope in a world that needs hope as much as it ever has.

In the face of change and destabilizing influences, it is even more critical that CBNPs be the agents of hope in a world that needs hope as much as it ever has. With approximately one-fifth of the 21st century already in the rear-view mirror, we need to have a solid reason for hope as we look to the future. This is not the kind of hope that is sometimes called wishful thinking. Hope is more than the reasonable anticipation of something good. Hope is about being convinced of a deferred certainty. It goes beyond unthinking optimism.

The opposite of hope is usually despair. Those who work in close proximity to people who have lost hope know what despair looks like. Yet the people who work or volunteer with community-based non-profits have to be purveyors of hope—not because they should deliver pithy, upbeat messages of positivity to those experiencing violence, discrimination, disenfranchisement, or the ravages of poverty, but because authentic hope is unbreakable in the face of the most profound challenges of life. More importantly, hope that has been dashed by the circumstances of life can be rekindled.

Isolation is the natural enemy of hope because isolated people are victims of a phenomenon that resembles torture. Throughout their history most CBNPs, just like their some of their clients, have isolated themselves in their own world. They have been hesitant to join forces or build partnerships with similar organizations. They were uniquely focused on their own issues in their own corner of a town or city. Sure, they would participate in round table discussions or attend formal meetings of similar non-profits in a neighbourhood or region. However, there was always this sense of being utterly alone in their own small area to combat the forces of darkness; a sentiment that was part of the mantra of almost every community organization that sought to do good work.

For hope to flourish, CBNPs must break out of their self-imposed isolation and develop workable partnerships that aim to bring real change to their towns, cities, and regions. When that happens, hope will replace cynicism, and real change will produce measurable outcomes. Good work will be replaced by work that delivers real solutions to the people in our communities who need accompaniment and support. In turn, many of the people who currently benefit from the services that are provided will be served more effectively. Good work will be done better. In the end, the ultimate vision of almost every CBNP should be that, some day, they will not have a lineup of clients at their door and that the services they currently offer will no longer be needed.

APPENDIX 1

The purpose of the grid is to summarize some of the ideas in the book using a simple table. Naturally, a simple table will not be fully explanatory. It provides, at a glance, key components of the messages contained in *Good Work Done Better*.

Past Versus Future of Community-Based Non-Profits

	PAST REALITY 20th century	FUTURE REALITY 21st century
Driver for policy development and funding decisions	Visibility and dramatic anecdotes	Reliable real-time data
Key aim of funders of community-based non-profits	Support community groups	Resolve social challenges
Government policy framework designed to respond to social concerns	Haphazard government initiatives tied to electoral cycles that focus on "patches"	Well-coordinated multi-level government policies that target outcomes
Behaviour of community-based non-profits	Lone ranger and protest organizer	Partner and advocate
Business model of community-based non-profits	Charity	Problem solving
The basis for the public's engagement in resolving social challenges	Myths and misperceptions: resulting in random acts of charity	Awareness and understanding: resulting in support for permanent solutions

APPENDIX 2
What can governments do? Three possible policy initiatives

Almost all really new ideas have a certain aspect of foolishness when they are first produced.
—**Alfred North Whitehead**

The premise of this appendix is that government-directed policy can make a difference. Policies and programs on their own will not resolve the challenges without a comprehensive movement that includes input from a wide group of stakeholders, including those who will benefit from the policies. Consensus with respect to the tactical approach is unlikely, but there are several bold moves that can be undertaken and that, if well-coordinated, can change the equation for many of the most vulnerable people and contribute to both social justice and economic progress.

An additional premise is that basic monetary support systems that address the fundamentals of food and housing will have a concomitant impact on many of the challenges related to child poverty, education, and some elements of gender-based discrimination. Fundamentally, the lack of economic power (having no money) and the absence of agency (feeling as if one has no choice in a situation) produce the potential for exploitation of women and children and any other vulnerable social group. The absence of economic freedom has been at the heart of many of the historical inequalities and injustices that have impacted indigenous peoples and a variety of racial minorities.

History has demonstrated that economic and social systems work best when everyone feels that they have an opportunity to progress or succeed. Human beings like to have a sense of participation in their destiny so that they own their options. People who feel cornered or excluded will not contribute to society in a meaningful way. When groups of disenfranchised or devalued people exist, it can become a recipe for subtle expressions of dissatisfaction that, in turn, become the catalyst for political unrest. When groups of people believe that they are being systematically excluded or devalued, or if ambition and optimism is replaced by hopelessness and cynicism, then it is only matter of time until the underpinnings of society begin to erode.

Therefore, it is incumbent on those who govern and senior level policy makers to address social issues. It isn't easy to eliminate complex social challenges. The initiatives in this appendix will not solve every complex social challenge. It will take many years and many steps to resolve issues that have emerged due to inequality, discrimination, racism, and misogyny. Nonetheless, it is critical that governments avoid defaulting to inaction or that they merely continue to invest money on responding only to the most compelling emergencies. Complex social problems can be resolved if the collective courage exists to face up to it and take the hard (and sometimes expensive) steps to fix it.

1. **Governments and policy framers need to identify and clearly define the causes and the parameters of specific complex social issues.** It is no longer good enough to respond to the symptoms of the moment or to pressure groups that generate the most noise. It is essential that the reasons why the issues exist be well understood so that the cause can be addressed. It is also essential that emergency responses be a component of a plan that includes longer-term solutions.

2. **The public needs to become better informed** and solutions need to be framed in a way that is easy to understand.

3. **Changes need to be made to non-profit funding models.** Expectations related to results and impact need to replace measurement of activities and programs. Community-based non-profits cannot continue to be run the way they have been run for the past 100 years if we expect them to deliver measurable outcomes that will alter the existing social equation.

4. **Time frames for policy deployment must be established that transcend electoral cycles.** Any complex problem that has been building in intensity for many years cannot be resolved in four years. Consensus across party lines and between levels of government will need to be constructed so that policies designed to bring long-term social stability are not impacted by changes in governments from election to election.

5. **Best practices that have produced results in other countries must be evaluated** and tested by funding carefully monitored pilot projects.

Three basic policy ideas that can be considered:

- **Guaranteed or universal minimum income –** discussed briefly during the review of social myths (Social Myth #1 – chapter four), the basic principle involves implementing a government-funded program to re-distribute tax dollars by providing monthly payments to individuals or families with income levels below a specified threshold. It is designed to raise incomes to a level whereby recipients can afford basic goods and services. It aims to reduce or eliminate some traditional government programs and may also reduce the demand for some non-profit social initiatives like food security services.

    DESIGNED TO: Reduce social inequality and simplify government support programs

    WHY: It aims to raise the standard of living for those on the margins and create a positive economic ripple effect by creating new consumers. It might lower longer-term social costs and reduce inequality of opportunity.

    WHY NOT: It provides a broad government-mandated income threshold and requires a significant investment and a massive re-orientation of social assistance programs such as welfare. It can create a disincentive for some people to seek lower paying traditional employment and is subject to considerable bureaucratic rule making and oversight to prevent abuses.

- **Managed urban housing subsidy –** an initiative that can be implemented in conjunction with supported housing programs for people who are re-entering housing or are housed precariously. Rather than providing money directly to the individual, a qualified non-profit agency is mandated to pay housing costs directly to a landlord for a prescribed time period. Funding is provided to non-profit agencies that are experienced and recognized housing experts in the community and includes a funding formula designed to allow the agency to provide psychosocial support systems to the client.

    DESIGNED TO: Facilitate the process of obtaining suitable permanent housing quickly in competitive rental markets for those who are experiencing homelessness or are ill equipped to maintain housing.

    WHY: It removes barriers to entry as landlords are guaranteed payment and recognize that the individual or family is receiving ongoing social support from a recognized community partner. It also targets funding and ensures that it is only used for housing.

WHY NOT: It may not be designed to last indefinitely and is not likely to be suitable for every person or situation. It is likely to be more effective in urban settings but requires program adjustments based on local conditions (rental market realities). It could also artificially inflate rental pricing. Requires government funding partnerships with a limited number of high-capacity agencies in order to generate critical mass potentially limiting universal access.

- **Housing and infrastructure building incentives** – a series of well-coordinated local policy initiatives that encourage the profitable construction of housing developments that are designed to incorporate a significant percentage of affordable units. Policies can include measures that are designed to encourage certain types of development or to limit factors like gentrification of some neighborhoods and the prevalence of housing stock being utilized as short-term rental units. It can include rules that limit an owner's ability to increase rents of tenants or engage in short-term rental opportunities.

  DESIGNED TO: Encourage new construction or renovation/redeployment of affordable housing units with a maximum of flexibility by providing specific incentives to land owners and developers.

  WHY: It can be designed to respond to specific needs at a local or regional level. It encourages the building of a variety of affordable housing units while avoiding the creation of government-managed low-income housing ghettos by creating a financial incentive for developers to construct mixed developments that meet a number of local needs. A broad range of incentives can include tax reduction, density waivers, and permit expediting.

  WHY NOT: It is challenging to redevelop areas within established neighbourhoods due to "not in my backyard" pressures. New residential projects can take years to construct, and the housing needs in a community can change by the time new units become available. If incentives fail to appeal to landlords and/or experienced local construction firms, they are seldom successful. Regulations that place restrictions on the usage of existing residences can cause property owners to find loopholes that allow them to maximize their return on investment to the detriment of the community as a whole.

APPENDIX 3
Developing an actionable checklist

The book proposes that the most effective way to usher in social change is by developing consensus and engaging multiple stakeholders in a broad movement. If we want to begin the process of moving in the right direction, it has to start with a coherent understanding of the issues. A good example of how the speed of change can accelerate around a large, complex issue is the recent emergence of the importance of the global challenge of climate change. For many years, it was only discussed by environmental activists and a few scientists. Politicians and the business community largely ignored it, and the public found it boring. However, in the past ten years, a broad consensus has begun to coalesce into a movement. Most people concur that a world that becomes just a bit warmer will be a world that may become increasingly uninhabitable. The broad movement that is taking shape is moving towards goals related to environmental sustainability. They are moving in that direction because of enlightened self-interest. People fear for their children's future. Governments are listening to warnings about cost of natural disasters and flooded coastlines. Businesses see the threat of the status quo and are discovering financial opportunities with emerging green technologies. One major global insurance company has declared that a world that is four degrees warmer will be uninsurable. As a result of this belief, they have undertaken a number of key actions to ensure that the business of insurance, their business, will continue to exist.

Similarly, the many complex social challenges we face in North America can be solved, but they require concerted and aligned efforts by multiple stakeholders. It will take a movement. It will take the ability for North Americans to envision how resolving social issues is in everyone's best interest and that it does not need to be expensive. In fact, doing nothing will be far more expensive.

Will Rogers once said that if you are on the right track, you will get run over if you just sit there. The purpose of this book is to elevate the dialogue and to encourage all of us to move into action by doing the right things in the right way. Being on the right track isn't enough. Good ideas, like good intentions, need to be followed by a series of well-crafted action steps. It is not enough to agree that it is time to do something to resolve complex social challenges. We each can, and should, do what needs to be done within our particular sphere of influence.

The actionable checklist below is not intended to be a "final to do list." Rather, it contains a series of possible starting points. As we suggested earlier in the book, if a manifesto is a problem stated in reverse, then perhaps some of these statements can serve to guide our future actions.

Governments:

☐ We will ensure that we coherently align policies and programs with the initiatives of other levels of government

☐ We will de-politicize the issue of resolving complex social challenges by removing partisanship from the policy-making process

☐ We will focus on long-term funding of solutions rather than linking programs to electoral cycles

☐ We will avoid the tendency to fund patches by insisting on data-driven decision making linked to defined long term outcomes

Funding Agencies:

☐ We will provide financial support based on an organization's potential to generate impact rather than on its ability to lobby for funding

☐ We will end the practice of assessing the effectiveness of CBNPs based primarily on financial ratios

☐ We will recognize the need for community-based non-profits to invest in infrastructure and engage qualified management in order to achieve results

☐ We will develop multi-year partnerships with CBNPs moving away from "project funding" and towards "outcome funding"

Media:

☐ We will develop a more comprehensive understanding of complex social issues by actively learning from subject matter experts and seeking to truly educate our audience

- ☐ We will refrain from profiling random acts of charity that are primarily donor-centric

- ☐ We will avoid the traps of partisan activism and thinly veiled scepticism, but we will continue to ask tough questions and require clear answers

- ☐ We will elevate the practice of telling real stories about the challenges and triumphs of real people without suggesting that all successes or tragedies are normative

The Public:

- ☐ We will identify a limited number of compelling causes and proactively develop an understanding of the realities of each one so that we can support them appropriately

- ☐ We will avoid acting independently or spontaneously and commit to providing regular, ongoing support to high-impact community-based non-profits that are at work in our community

- ☐ We will lend our voice to support policies that will shift the equation away from temporary "patches" and towards permanent solutions that produce a measurable impact

CBNPs:

- ☐ We will commit to developing solutions and longer-term outcomes for those we serve—as opposed to investing energy to highlight our own needs

- ☐ We will take a long, hard look at our operations and programs to determine if we are producing measurable results or merely running programs

- ☐ We will avoid the narrative that suggests that more money is the primary answer that will help us address long-standing complex social issues

- ☐ We will stop using guilt and shame to motivate donors and start communicating messages of hope and potential

- ☐ We will review and, if necessary, overhaul our board structures and processes to elevate the practice of good governance

- ☐ We will acknowledge that doing good work simply isn't good enough

APPENDIX 4
Is a Pandemic a Potential Disruptor?

In late February 2020, while reviewing the final draft of this book, I did a quick word search to see if there was any reference to a pandemic. We were beginning to hear information daily about the rapid spread of COVID-19. Interestingly, the word "pandemic" had been used only once in the original manuscript. This is not a huge surprise, given that the topics in this book are unrelated to global pandemics. The one reference in the original manuscript was in a section where the merits of a charitable approach are being applauded in specific circumstances like disasters or pandemics. We have subsequently added a reference to the COVID-19 reality in the introduction and in a number of other pertinent places. The global pandemic has been responsible for a number of major shifts in the way people and organizations are responding to community needs. These shifts may prove interesting as the economies in the western hemisphere recover, and life begins to return to a new version of normal.

Back in 2017, I was in a meeting with the health minister of the province where I live. The purpose of the meeting was to outline the reality that a number of front-line organizations were providing quite a few basic healthcare services to the homeless population, and that our donors were covering the costs. Our proposition was that the government-funded health care system in Canada ought to be funding these services. The minister reviewed our costs, and looked at us somewhat sheepishly. He asked if we were suggesting that all of us around the table should simply become "employees of the state." It was an interesting question, and one that was asked largely as a way of implying that non-profit agencies ought to be content with the minimal levels of funding we were being granted, unless we were ready to turn our operations over to the Ministry of Health. Memories of this meeting came back to me during recent discussions with our local elected officials—discussions that were completely different in their content. Clearly, the COVID-19 pandemic will change the landscape. The realities of a health crisis that threatens the poor and the vulnerable creates an obvious need for a close partnership between healthcare organizations and front-line organizations. Arguably, front-line organizations ARE healthcare organizations. What is more fundamental to basic health and wellness than food and shelter?

For the last few months, humankind has lived through a series of events that are virtually unprecedented. The realities of the COVID-19 pandemic have touched almost every person and every country on the planet. Information has changed rapidly and governments have had to respond to an ever-evolving situation. Some public officials and health care leaders responded rapidly and decisively, while others did not. Undoubtedly, lessons will be extracted and theories will be developed for many years to come, as experts review the decision-making processes that were employed by the leaders who were tasked with responding to the crisis. This appendix does not pretend to analyze the principles of crisis management, nor does it intend to offer any opinions on what was done or not done to respond to the pandemic. The goal of this section is to highlight one observation. It is an observation that has profound implications for the community-based non-profit sector.

Key Observation: During the COVID-19 pandemic, many CBNPs were considered "essential services." This raises an important question. If a particular CBNP is delivering essential services during a pandemic, is it not delivering essential services in normal times?

In March 2020, in keeping with a number of government directives, members of the public changed their daily routines and moved into survival mode, trying to follow recommendations that aimed to limit the community-level transmission of this new virus. The need for social distancing forced some community organizations to stop operating. Other CBNPs could not continue to function due to constraints related to the availability of volunteers. As the crisis became more acute in mid-March, many CBNPs' services were curtailed by government order. Operations like face-to-face counselling services, free dental clinics, thrift shops, and day centers either reduced their services drastically, or closed altogether. At the same time, other community-based non-profit organizations were designated as essential services and were expected to continue, or even accelerate, operations. Services like the operation of food banks, and help to those experiencing homelessness all became critical. Workers who provide care for seniors and the mobility challenged were recognized for their important service. The public's understanding of the diverse components that contribute to healthcare and wellness expanded.

In Canada, most traditional healthcare services are publicly-funded. In the USA, the cost of healthcare for most people is covered by private insurance or by public programs like Medicare. Americans are divided on the concept of universal healthcare coverage, whereas in Canada, it is seen as a fundamental component of the Canadian identity. At the heart of this debate is the concept of an essential service. Is it not strange that we all agree that services like fire protection in most of our cities, American or Canadian, are essential services that need to be collectively funded? Fire departments do not normally have to appeal to the public to obtain donations so that they can pay their staff and operate their equipment. In most parts of North America, support for fire departments and firefighters is provided by tax dollars. Most communities do not have to raise money to purchase the essentials that are required to provide something that we've defined for years as an emergency service.

So then, why shouldn't governments provide adequate recurring funding to CBNPs that deliver essential services? In a post-COVID-19 world, will the essential services that CBNPs provide no longer be dependent upon their ability to secure donations to fund their operations? Will this terrible pandemic be the catalyst for an overhaul of how services to the disenfranchised and vulnerable are delivered? Is this the disruptor that will drive historic change? Will the new-found visibility of the essential role of CBNPs result in the reorientation of some services? Will it be a catalyst for the establishment of new standards of care that result in improved funding partnerships between governments and CBNPs? Will some of the services currently delivered by CBNPs be absorbed into a fully-funded healthcare system?

ACKNOWLEDGEMENTS

Any book of this sort is always the product of multiple influences and thousands of conversations. It is important to humbly acknowledge that many wise and knowledgeable people have generously shared their thoughts with me over the past few years. Many of your thoughts and ideas helped shape the contents of this book. I cannot possibly mention all of the friendships and mentorships that have been a huge blessing on my journey so far. Some of the thinking of a number of my colleagues has undoubtedly influenced this book. In addition, a variety of people have provided extraordinary encouragement, support, and generosity. You know who you are. This book would not have happened without you. In any book there will be misstatements, errors, or gaps. Those are entirely my responsibility. The following people have been particularly inspiring, and I am deeply grateful to them.

My wife, **Susan Kaiser***, the best partner anyone could have and my biggest cheerleader. She isn't only a talented lawyer; she is also a wise counsellor who offered a variety of valuable insights and ideas that have vastly improved this manuscript.*

My daughters, **Dominique** *and* **Rachel***, who provide me with daily inspiration, and who tolerated the fact that I spent almost every Saturday, for about a year, chained to my computer to distil the ideas for this book. They are both incredibly talented young ladies who care deeply about the vulnerable and the disenfranchised.*

Matthew Pearce*, who has served as CEO of Old Brewery Mission in Montreal for many years. Matthew's ideas have contributed in countless ways to the key ideas in this book. In the face of considerable opposition by some well-established groups, he has been relentless in his quest to re-frame the understanding of homelessness and the solutions that are required to address it. I consider Matthew to be the "dean" of our Montreal network of organizations that are in the process of changing the equation.*

Francois Boissy*, CEO of Maison du Père, who is an innovator and valued advisor. Francois exudes the kind of joy and competence that every leader should have. He refuses to accept the status quo and has a solution-oriented mindset.*

Dozens of elected officials have been extremely influential in helping me understand the complexities of developing and implementing policy. They include good friends like the Honourable **Marc Miller***, the Honourable* **David Lametti***, and the Honourable* **Denis**

Coderre. I consider these three gentlemen examples of politicians who deeply care about those in need and who lead by serving others. They are not alone. There are thousands of others who work hard on behalf of their constituents.

Dr. Karl Moore, who wrote the foreword. Karl is one of the quickest thinkers you will ever encounter. He was captivated by the "big idea" of the book, and he was instrumental in validating some of its essential components. Karl is a leading strategic thinker and leadership expert in academia. He is also a man of principle who is not afraid to have a little bit of fun. I'll never forget when I saw him as I was in a line-up to attend a rock concert. Without missing a beat, he said, "Sam, I had no idea that you were nearly cool enough to attend a Bryan Adams concert."

Cyril Morgan, my predecessor at Welcome Hall Mission. His tenacity positioned the organization to develop the disciplines and processes that are essential to the "problem solving" approach that was adopted.

My lifelong friend **John Hall**, a graduate of INSEAD and a seasoned business professional. John has encouraged me, corrected me, and completed my sentences for more than 50 years. He was also never afraid to give me tough advice when I was sure I didn't need it!

Enzo Gabrielli, who has extensive understanding of the board/management relationship in his capacity at Horizon Capital. He was eager and willing to review the chapter of this book that addresses board governance to review the ideas and recommendations and ensure that they are reasonable.

The entire team at **FriesenPress**, who handled the editing and proofreading to design and promotion. They are real professionals. They have provided the essential blend of guidance and creative liberty that has made this book better.

Finally, I am deeply indebted to the **outstanding team of people who are my colleagues at Welcome Hall Mission. These people** serve unselfishly and demonstrate unparalleled devotion to the vision to participate in the transformation of our city. Along with hundreds of dedicated volunteers and valuable donors, they are responsible for the care and accompaniment that we provide to the thousands of clients we serve. They live the Mission's brand promise of **Shelter, Food, Love** every day.

ABOUT THE AUTHOR

Sam Watts serves at a large community-based non-profit organization in Montreal, Canada. Unlike many CBNP leaders—he spent the majority of his career in the private sector. Previous to joining the Mission, he held a number of management positions in the business community and, for fourteen years, worked with leaders of large corporations as a performance improvement consultant.

Watts has written dozens of articles on leadership and management, and has had the privilege of speaking to groups in more than a dozen countries on four continents. He resides in Beaconsfield, Quebec.

CPSIA information can be obtained
at www.ICGtesting.com
Printed in the USA
BVHW010150260720
584663BV00007B/11